The Final Quarter

Make the rest of your life
the best of your life!

≈≈≈

Sue Heath

The Final Quarter
Copyright © 2018 by Sue Heath

All rights reserved. No part of this book may be reproduced or transmitted in any form or by any means without written permission from the author.

Unless otherwise noted, all Scripture quotations are from the NIV, Holy Bible, New International Version®, NIV® Copyright ©1973, 1978, 1984, 2011 by Biblica, Inc.® Used by permission. All rights reserved worldwide. Scripture quotations marked NKJV are taken from the New King James Version®. Copyright © 1982 by Thomas Nelson. Used by permission. All rights reserved. Scripture quotations marked KJV are taken from the King James Version of the Holy Bible. Scripture quotations marked TLB are taken from The Living Bible copyright © 1971 by Tyndale House Foundation. Used by permission of Tyndale House Publishers Inc., Carol Stream, Illinois 60188. All rights reserved. Scripture quotations marked NLT are taken from *Holy Bible*, New Living Translation, copyright © 1996, 2004, 2015 by Tyndale House Foundation. Used by permission of Tyndale House Publishers, Inc., Carol Stream, Illinois 60188. All rights reserved.

ISBN 978-1724572325

Printed in USA

Dedication

I want to dedicate this book to Gene—my husband, lover, best friend, and fellow traveler on this journey of life. We have celebrated fifty-two years of marriage so far, and survived all the traumas, turmoil, hurts, disappointments, and pain that go with this blending of lives called marriage. We've also experienced times of joy, fun, learning, new experiences, traveling, and just enjoying the comfort of each other's presence. I'm thankful we both stayed the course, as our relationship is stronger as a result.

I also dedicate this book to our two sons, Brent and Kurt, who have been a great source of joy and friendship. They have filled our lives with sports, friends, wives, and grandkids—who are another source of much excitement and fun! Our family vacations have been memory-making times, which we will always treasure.

Finally, I want to include my three sisters—Pat, Ann, and Becky. They have been with me from the beginning, and as we've matured, we have become best friends and one another's staunch supporters. We have shared joys, sorrows, and struggles as we've each lived our lives in different areas of the US. Thank goodness for our sister retreats to reconnect in a stronger way and share laughter and talks. We must include our husbands, as they wouldn't know what to do with themselves while we are out having fun!

Table of Contents

Foreword 7
Preface 11
Introduction 15

Part 1: The First Quarter **19**
Chapter 1: First Quarter of Life—The Start 21

Part 2: The Second Quarter **31**
Chapter 2: Second Quarter—The Development 33

Part 3: The Third Quarter **51**
Chapter 3: Third Quarter—The Refining 53
Chapter 4: Early Dreams and New Passions 65
Chapter 5: Vital Relationships 85

Part 4: The Final Quarter **107**
Chapter 6: Fourth Quarter—The Finishing 109
Chapter 7: Challenges Faced in Aging 117
Chapter 8: Spirit: Our First Aspect of "Being" 129
Chapter 9: Soul—Emotional and Mental Mind-sets:
    Our Second Aspect of "Being" 137
Chapter 10: Body: Our Third Aspect of "Being" 147
Chapter 11: What Is Your Legacy? 169
Chapter 12: Finishing Well 181

Notes 87
About the Author 189

Foreword

The Final Quarter . . . How do we know when we're there? In a perfect scenario we would live to be a hundred years old and experience all that a long life provides. I like to think that will be the case for all of you, but my question is: Are you living your life to its fullest *now*? If tomorrow isn't promised, are you giving this life the best of you in the current moment?

As an international speaker and transformation expert, I have been blessed to meet people from all walks of life and experience. As I travel the world speaking to people from different levels of society and achievement, I find that many people are only *going through* this life instead of *being* in this life. Most have yet to tap into their true value within and the manifestation of the purpose they will serve while they are alive. The late Dr. Miles Monroe said:

> The wealthiest place in the world is not the gold mines of South America or the oil fields of Iraq or Iran. They are not the diamond mines of South Africa or the banks of the world. The wealthiest place on the planet is just down the road. It is the cemetery. There lie buried companies that were never started, inventions that were never made, bestselling books that were never written, and masterpieces that were never painted. In the cemetery is buried the greatest treasure of untapped potential.[1]

In my travels I also meet amazing people who have broken the mold, who are living out their potential in life. As we go through life, we will pass by some people, never knowing their plight or their passion. Yet others will stand out forever in our minds and hearts. The author of this book happens to be one of those people for me.

I have always been a big networker, attending events of all types, shaking hands, and increasing my sphere of influence. At these networking events, my focus is to search out and connect with people of influence. In most cases, these people of influence reveal themselves quickly. The way they carry themselves and the presence they exhibit is the dead giveaway. Sue Heath stood out to me immediately. She carried an aura around her that was undeniable. She exemplified grace, confidence, and peace.

After getting to know her better and understanding the true depth of her life experience, it became evident to me that Sue would leave her mark and impact this world in a big way. She had already done so much—raising a family, reaching the pinnacles of a successful nursing career, being a driven entrepreneur, and giving her heart and soul selflessly on the mission fields of the world. What impressed me the most was that she was entering her final quarter . . . and she was just getting started!

In *The Final Quarter* Sue Heath takes us on a journey of tears and triumph, passion and purpose. She provides all of us with the inspiration and guidance to "make the rest of our life the best of our life." I know I am personally elated about the millions of lives this book will impact, and I am thankful that I was blessed with the opportunity to play a small role in helping it become a reality. I encourage you, as you begin this journey with Sue, to open your mind and heart to receive everything this book can and will provide.

Mind, body, and spirit means that our well-being comes not only from physical health but from mental and spiritual health as well. To be "healthy," we must pay attention to all three aspects of our nature—mind, body, and spirit. To live and perform at our fullest potential in this life we must treat every day as if we are in *The Final Quarter.*

God bless you on your journey…

Steve Hopper
Motivational Speaker, Author, Transformation Expert
SteveHopperInternational.com

Preface

Have you ever wondered if your life has made a lasting impact or delivered value to others? Do you ever step back and evaluate it? I invite you to join me in *The Final Quarter* to see how I decided to approach these powerful questions. Whatever stage of life you are in today, we all age, so decide *now* how you want to finish your run in this life.

This book is not about dying or being close to dying, but rather to celebrate all that we have learned, accomplished, and experienced up to this point, and to focus on living every minute we have left to the fullest of our ability. This book has been created for a time such as this.

This book is dedicated to all of us entering the last phase of our lives; we are entering those golden years that we've heard about but not experienced—until now. Perhaps our parents have passed on and we are now the last generation of our family.

At certain moments in my life I've thought, *Oh no, now I'm the old person. Am I the next in line to die? What was my life all about? What will people remember me for? Will anyone come to my funeral? What will my family do without me?*

If you are anything like me, you are beginning to see and experience the physical impacts of getting older. I know personally that many of these could have been prevented if I'd taken better care of myself through diet and exercise. The good news is, we can do some things even now to improve our longevity. In the pages of this book I will share these with you.

Now that we have become part of the older generation, what do we do with ourselves? What is our role at this point? Do we hang up our hats and just sit around, letting life pass us by since we can't move as fast anymore? Or do we have other options? If you have ever asked any of these questions, then you are in the right place. In *The Final Quarter* I will share my ideas and experiences with you about these questions. My hope is that what you read will give you inspiration and hope for a vital and productive final quarter.

Having recently reached the ripe age of seventy-five years old, I began to look at my life in quarters, much like a football game.

> First quarter: birth to twenty-five years of age
> Second quarter: twenty-six to fifty
> Third quarter: fifty-one to seventy-five
> Fourth quarter: seventy-six to one hundred

Since I now have one foot edging toward the last quarter, I decided to take stock of several different aspects of my life:

- Who have I developed into because of my experiences over the years?
- What do I want to be when I grow up?
- What do I want to accomplish while I'm here?
- What have I given to the world to make it better?
- What values have I instilled in my family?
- Have I loved so that my loved ones know they have been much loved?
- Do I just have to sit back and retire because of my age, or is it okay to keep going?
- What do I do with all the energy I still have?
- What do I do with the life lessons, knowledge, and wisdom I've gained in my lifetime?
- Who can I invest my life in?
- Do I have to take a backseat and let all the younger people have their place in the sun?

- Have I let God be the foundation of my life, and guide my decisions and direction in life?

So many questions. So I decided to evaluate where I've been and where I am going. I wanted to look back at my formative years and see how they impacted who I have become. To identify the moments and choices that guided me, I took each quarter, examined events during those years, and found the *defining moments*.

Maybe you have struggled with these questions as well. No matter your age, I encourage you to take a deep look at your life too. Our days are numbered, but we don't know how many we have left—only God does. Perhaps we should consider that *we are all* in our last quarter of life and live each day as though it could be our last!

I have personally completed this evaluation and I can tell you that it is life changing. In the pages of *The Final Quarter*, I break down the blueprint that gave me clarity regarding where I have been and where I am going. And just maybe, the answers you seek can be found within these pages as well.

Sue Heath

Introduction

You hold this book in your hand because I was challenged. I was challenged to share why at seventy-five years old I am still so passionate about meeting new people, going to network meetings, and sharing with others my knowledge about the alternative health field. I was challenged to share my stories about traveling to other countries and cultures to give others a message of hope, health, and healing.

I know now that I received this challenge to encourage *and remind you* that no matter your age, you too can keep on doing, being, going, sharing, traveling, and loving with a stronger passion than ever before.

In 2014 I retired from my "professional" career, so I could have time for my "passionate" career.

I didn't want any regrets to follow me to the grave, so I decided to live each day I was given to its fullest potential. I understood that we do not have to sit back and pass our days in mindless retired pleasure—especially when we are wired to serve. The world needs us . . . people need our wisdom, our experience, and our knowledge.

This book is about staying in the game of life. And if you do, it will keep you younger—longer! This book is about making your last quarter count for something.

> *Just remember, once you're over the hill you begin to*
> *pick up speed.*
> —Arthur Schopenhauer

On marketwatch.com, Jack Tatar, a financial advisor, wrote a blog in which he shared the five biggest regrets of retirees:

- I wish I had saved more money.
- I wish I had been more knowledgeable about money and/or had a trusted financial advisor to work with.
- I wish I had taken better care of my health.
- I wish I had gotten involved in the things I really love sooner in life.
- I wish I had spoken sooner with my children about the needs and desires for my later life.[2]

In Bronnie Ware's book *The Top Five Regrets of the Dying: A Life Transformed by the Dearly Departed*, she shared five themes she learned from her patients. She then also shared solutions for those regrets—ways to avoid falling into the same traps in your own life.[3]

Regret #1: I wish I'd had the courage to live a life true to myself, not the life others expected of me.

This number-one regret reminds us not to give up too many of our dreams to please others. Ware reminds us to honor our dreams, because when our health suffers, it's too late. We must live our dreams while our health gives us the freedom to do so.

Regret #2: I wish I hadn't worked so hard.

We can live a simpler life that requires less income than we may think we need. Simplifying and being conscious of our choices makes it possible to live a full and happy life with less income. Then we have more time for new opportunities and we have happier lives.

Regret #3: I wish I'd had the courage to express my feelings.

Ware notes that many people carry bitterness and resentment as a result of holding their feelings in and opting to keep quiet just to keep the peace. This bitterness can actually lead to physical illness. If this is you, remember that you can only control your own reactions to situations, not others' reactions. Learn to speak truthfully to others, and even if their initial response may be difficult, eventually your relationships will grow healthier. Or you will be able to let go of the unhealthy ones.

Regret #4: I wish I'd stayed in touch with my friends.

Often we get so busy and no longer keep in touch with old friends, and over time relationships grow distant. Then, as we age, we find ourselves lonely. It is not easy to nurture relationships, and the older we are the harder it becomes, partly because our health can begin to limit our opportunities to get out and spend time with friends. Ware notes in her book that love and relationships are the most important priorities near the end of our lives.

Regret #5: I wish I'd let myself be happier.

Finally, at the end of life, people recognize that their own happiness is their choice, not the result of a lifestyle or a collection of material possessions. Most people, at the end of their lives, wish they had laughed more, and desire to have a more carefree, happy attitude, not caring what other people think. So why not make the choice to be happy while time is still left.

Why wait until the end to express your regret? If you identify with any of these regrets now, you have time to correct the situation and create a more positive, inspirational, and joyful final quarter of life.

The Final Quarter

In addition to examining my defining moments through three quarters, and reflecting on ways to eliminate regret, as I looked back over my life, I discovered seven stages to create a meaningful final quarter of life. Along the way throughout this book, you'll find out how to consider these stages as you seek to finish your life well:

- Path
- Purpose
- Presents
- Place
- Preparation
- Perseverance
- Passion

If we are willing to learn from other people's experiences and apply that knowledge to our own lives, it will save us from making some of the same mistakes. My hope is that the experiences and knowledge passed on to you in this book will do just that. Not only can it prevent some of the mistakes others and I have made but it will also empower you to make the fourth quarter of your life the best quarter of your life. Let's get started!

The First Quarter

Ages 1–25

This time of your life is foundational, usually setting the course your life path will take. It's a time of moving from childhood into young adulthood, culminating in education, college, vocational choices, and even spousal choices. For many it's also a time of starting families and careers. Defining moments in this first quarter help guide you toward your life's path.

Chapter 1
First Quarter of Life—The Start 1943–68

I was born in July 1943 to Felix and Alberta Walker, the second daughter out of four girls. I was a sunny little thing so I'm *sure* I brought my parents much joy. To keep track of us girls, when talking to others about us, my mom referred to us as Number 1, who was Pat; Number 2, Sue; Number 3, Ann; and Number 4, Becky. Even with five years between most of us, she couldn't keep us straight.

We lived in Garrett, an old railroad town in northeast Indiana. My father was the pastor of the Christian Church. Being a preacher's kid (PK) meant everyone watched your behavior and expected you to be little angels. Of course, we often failed miserably. I'd sit next to some girlfriends in church and giggle over something silly. Since my dad was in the pulpit, he could see what we were doing. After the service we were all called into his office and given a "talking-to." As a result, we had to take notes during the next sermon and report what we had learned. To this day, I couldn't tell you what I learned—except how to take good notes when someone was talking! It always felt like our family was held to a higher standard and watched to see that we upheld it.

The Final Quarter

My mom taught piano and organ lessons, so I took care of my two younger sisters, Ann and Becky, while Pat, my older sister, worked at a secretarial job outside the home. That meant I helped with meals and housework and became a responsible young teenager. When Becky, the youngest, was born, I often had to take care of her as I was ten years older. Once when I was holding her while she drank from her bottle, she choked, and I panicked! I didn't know what to do, so Daddy had to take her and pat her on the back. I thought I had almost killed my little sister by letting her drink too fast. All I could do was cry from sheer fear.

Mom tried to teach all her girls how to play the piano, but I was rebellious. If I had to do so much housework and take care of siblings, I certainly didn't want to also practice piano. So, after a long time of trying, my mom finally threw her hands up and said, "Okay, I'm done. You don't have to learn." I felt relieved at the time, but in later years I regretted my choice. It saddened me that I didn't know how to express myself through music. Two of my other sisters became accomplished pianists and played for church and special services, and even taught piano lessons to students.

At one point, Mom went away for two weeks to take piano theory classes with Fred Waring in Pennsylvania. She left me in charge of fixing meals, watching sisters, and also a load of canning beans. Have you ever used one of those big canners with the jiggling metal piece on the top? Our canner always made me fear it would explode so I was afraid to be left alone in the same room with it. I don't know how, but I did manage to get through that traumatic canning experience intact and take all those finished jars out to cool.

My biggest joy was to read, so we girls would walk to the public library to load up on books every week. We'd struggle home with our arms piled with five to six books each. I loved reading all kinds of books—mysteries; Nancy Drew; science fiction; stories about

Chapter 1

nursing, missionaries, history, animals, and explorers. I even got caught in class one day when the teacher called on me to answer a question but I had not heard her, as I was reading a book beside me. My book was taken away. Bummer!

A defining moment from my childhood happened around the age of ten. One day while bike riding with another girl, I hit a big rock and fell, knocking my front teeth through my top lip and chipping them off. I vividly remember sitting on the road and crying my eyes out. I could feel my teeth were badly chipped and that scared me, as did my bleeding lip. The other girl just stood and looked at me in shock; she didn't know what to do for me. Since she wasn't helping me, and no one came out to see what was wrong, I finally decided to get up and make it back to her house. When we got to her house, they called my parents to come get me.

Because of my age, the dentist wouldn't cap my teeth until I was sixteen, saying they needed to get more mature in size. If you can imagine having two front teeth looking like fangs—an inverted V—that's what my teeth looked like. As a result, I kept my head down and wouldn't talk much to people. With a lisp, scar, and Dutch-boy haircut, I wanted to be invisible. Book reading became my escape and my salvation.

I would not realize until much later in life that this defining moment impacted my life in a negative way for years to come. The confidence I lacked throughout my life was greatly associated with this experience. I heard a motivational speaker say one time that most people do not live at their fullest potential in life because an adolescent is driving the car. In other words, the lack of confidence I experienced as an adult derived from the ten-year-old with broken teeth.

≈≈≈

Stage One to a Meaningful Final Quarter: *Path*

Throughout the book I will describe seven stages to create a meaningful final quarter. The first of these is *path*. The journey to find our path may include places, people, experiences, and interests. Where you are, the circumstances you experience, the areas of life you are drawn to—all these begin to give you a direction in life. God uses people and experiences to set your feet on the path He has designed for you. As you begin to identify your path, you will discover that others have likely gone before you to prepare the way.

What is the path of your life? What destination has God prepared for you to walk toward throughout your life and to finish well in your final quarter?

As a pastor's family, we frequently had missionaries visit our church or home for a meal and share their stories with us. As I listened to exciting tales, I desperately wanted to experience some of the same adventures they'd had. They talked about fitting into other cultures, learning the languages, and living life with people in foreign lands. Those stories sparked my interest, and one night while reading by the streetlight that poured in through my bedroom window, it was as though God spoke to my heart. I knew from the bottom of my heart that I was going to be either a nurse or missionary. All the stories I had read about nursing just drew me to want to take care of people and help them. I wanted to serve people by ministering to their needs and do it here in the US as well as someday in other countries. This night would be a defining moment for my *path*, as I knew with every fiber of my being that my life course was set.

Maybe you can relate to one or more of these *defining moments* in your life. What defining moment in your younger life set your path for life? These are the moments that have the most impact on our course in life.

If we are paying attention to our lives, we'll recognize those defining moments. The challenge for so many of us is that we are so deep into daily distractions and "being busy, busy" that we miss out on those moments and opportunities that—if jumped on—would get our careers and personal lives to a whole new level of wow.
—Robin S. Sharma

As I grew older, into my teen years, I wanted to put feet to my dream, so I worked as a candy striper in the hospital while a sophomore and junior in high school. We wore striped uniforms and little caps, so patients could distinguish us from the real thing. It's not a sight you see in hospitals much anymore, if at all. I got a taste of working with patients, handing out water, delivering flowers, giving back rubs to get patients ready for bed, and just experiencing hospital life. I loved it—the smell of a hospital, the sounds, working with the nurses and doctors, interacting with people, doing acts of service, helping to relieve the loneliness and feelings of helplessness many patients showed. I knew this was my purpose, what I was created for, as God gave me a servant heart to help others.

In 1961, after high school, I left to study nursing in Indianapolis at Methodist Hospital School of Nursing. The first two years we all had to live in the dorms. At times I had my own room; other times I shared one. But during my last year, I roomed with my good friend,

The Final Quarter

Susie, at an old hotel that was converted to rooms for the senior nurses. We would sunbathe on the roof and watch people below us on the streets. I confess we even threw water balloons a couple of times when we were being ornery!

Susie's dad was head of the ob-gyn department, so we often snuck up there to watch deliveries and tease the interns and residents. One night, a couple of them put us in a cart loaded with hospital gowns and towels. They rolled us down the halls, into the elevator, and down to the morgue. On the elevator, an evening supervisor asked them what they were doing. They told her they had to take some laundry down to the laundry department. It was all we could do to stifle our laughter and not get caught. To say we had fun during those years is an understatement.

Sometimes we worked nights, and after getting off work we'd go home to the dorm and sleep for several hours before getting up for classes, and then work again. One night we just couldn't get to sleep so we each took a sleeping pill. I put rollers in my hair each night so I'd look good for work, as we wore starched caps and looked like nurses. Susie told me to hurry up because the pills worked fast. I woke up hours later to find half my hair in curlers and water spilled on the bed—I hadn't worked fast enough before the pill knocked me out. Can you say, "Disaster hair?!"

After Susie and I graduated, we both worked in the OR/surgery department. One day we had gone to her house after work for dinner with her parents. We spent the night there, but overslept and had to rush to get out the door and to work on time. We both were struggling to get our uniforms on, curlers out of our hair, and makeup on. We piled into her car, she put it into reverse, and we slammed into her brother's car, knocking off his front bumper! We set it back on his car and hurried on to work, laughing like crazy the whole way. I don't know if he was laughing when he came out to see his car. Nursing school years were such fun, and I will never forget them.

I graduated from the last three-year diploma program in nursing in 1963, as the American Association of Nursing went on to make it a full bachelor of science program. As a result, I got lots of bedside experience rather than all the book learning they instituted in a degree program.

The first quarter of life brings the first taste of independence as well. Many of us decide to push the boundaries when finally given the chance. When I went to nursing school, I found freedom from all the rules at home and tried all the things that were not allowed when I was growing up:

- Smoking—one puff was enough for me.
- Drinking—couldn't stand the taste of beer, wine, or liquor).
- Dancing—*loved* that.
- Playing cards—played lots of fun games.
- Going to movies—another thing I enjoyed, especially since that's where I met Gene, my husband-to-be, on a triple date. I went with one of his fraternity brothers, Gene (who drove) and his date, along with another couple from their fraternity. We all went to see *Mutiny on the Bounty*. This was back in the days when you dressed up to go somewhere, so we girls dressed up in dresses and heels. He said he looked down the row and liked my *nose* and knew I was the girl for him.

When I met Gene, he was attending Butler University. He was from a farm in Fort Wayne, Indiana. When he took me home to meet his parents, they said they were so glad he found a blue-eyed girl. He and many of his family members had brown eyes, as did some of his former girlfriends. That made me feel good because a popular song around that time that was "Beautiful, Beautiful Brown Eyes," and I felt so deprived because I had *blue* eyes.

We dated for a year and half, then were engaged for a year and half. I worked in surgery while Gene finished college. After he graduated in 1966, we got married. I was just a month shy of twenty-three—still too young to be getting married, but I was in love with him. I knew he was an honest, honorable guy, and a good singer. Plus, I knew he would make a great father. Not long after our wedding, we moved down to Chapel Hill, North Carolina, so Gene could get his degree in public health.

During our engagement, while Gene was still at Butler, I worked in the surgery department of the Methodist Hospital as a circulating nurse. The OR was my home turf. I loved neuro cases and was often able to scrub in to teach new technicians how to handle these cases. You had to be fast with presenting the sutures, hemostats, and sponges to keep up with the surgeons. They could be demanding and impatient because they were dealing with serious areas of the brain and spinal cord. Every step in the surgical procedure could mean life or death to the patient.

The challenge, pace, stressful surgeries, being on call, routines we had to go through—all were like food to me; I ate it up! I remember one day rolling a cart with trays of surgical instruments into a surgery room, but the wheels caught on the door lintel and I tripped over—cart and all the instruments! I was embarrassed, and then frantic to get the instruments back into the sterilizer to redo them for the operation. That was not one of my finer days.

I think God must put that sense of real caring in my heart to be able to handle all the physical things that nurses have to take care of, as well as the hard work and long hours. If you go into nursing as *just a job*, it shows in your care and handling of people and will wear you out faster. The patients will notice it as well. I can see how

God prepared me for many aspects of nursing through all those early days of household chores and caring for my younger sisters. That helped set me on the path I was meant to travel in life.

How about you? What path were you set on early in your life? What drew your interest and sparked your dreams? Did you follow that interest by pursuing education in that passion, and were you fortunate enough to find a job in that same interest so you could help support yourself and family?

Or maybe you feel you never had a drawing to a particular job or career. My belief is that we are all unique and have been given a gift or gifts to utilize throughout life. God has given us everything we need to function in the purpose He created us for. Why not look back at your childhood to see if any incidents or defining moments could speak to this question. What did you like to do or want to do as a young child? Maybe it was just a faint stirring of interest. Take out that seed of an idea and examine it again. Does it still capture your heart's desire or interest? Dust off that dream and put some feet to it now. It's never too late.

Your work is going to fill a large part of your life, and also the only way to be truly satisfied is to do what you believe is great work. And the only way to do great work is to love what you do. If you haven't found it yet, keep looking. Don't settle. As with all matters of the heart, you'll know when you find it.
—Steve Jobs

The Second Quarter
Ages 26–50

The second quarter of life is *productive*, "full of living time"— growing our families and careers, finding side interests and hobbies, discovering how hormones play a big role in our life cycles as many women enter menopause, finding "tools" to use as we possibly join a career with a passion. While this quarter seems to be a time of stress; family focus; career building; and serving church, family, business, and nation, it can also begin to reveal greater purpose in life.

Chapter 2

Second Quarter—The Development 1968–93

In 1968, after Gene got his degree in public health, we moved to Mountaintop, Pennsylvania. He went to work for a gas and water utility company in the Wilkes-Barre and Scranton area. These were mining communities, but beautiful, with mountains all around. We found an old house, and after remodeling, it became our first home in the mountains. It stood on a corner lot with a big hill and an old three-level garage. The former owners raised rabbits there, so the garage had cubbyholes all over. The property also had an outhouse, which we decided to tear down. Didn't quite fit our outdoor décor!

Gene's job included a lot of outdoor work, so we got to visit manmade dams, go hiking in the woods, and travel around beautiful lakes. Enjoying nature became a fun family activity once we had our boys.

I worked in one of the area hospitals as a floor nurse until I became pregnant. I asked God to give us a boy. I knew I didn't want daughters, after living with three sisters, and experiencing what little girls were like. My sister Ann had a playmate over for "tea" one day. They had water and crackers—on *my* bed. Of course, they spilled the water, which upset me. Just dealing with the moods and hormones of the female species, I decided I didn't want to have to deal with them in our children. And you don't have to remind me that I'm a female. After living in a home where even our pets were female, I decided one female in the house was enough!

When I was four months along in my pregnancy, I quit work to prepare for a newborn—painting a crib, gathering supplies and clothes, and setting up a nursery. In 1970 our first son was born, Brent. He was a delight, so sixteen months later in 1971 we added our second son, Kurt, to complete our family. God was so good to hear my heart's cry for boys.

Our two sons were precious little guys and brought great joy to our lives. Being so close in age, they always had a playmate and got along quite well. We made the enclosed front porch their playroom. It was almost always strewn with their building blocks, Legos, little toy cars, toy soldiers, stuffed animals, and "boy" toys. They brought an added dimension to our family that enhanced it greatly. Several neighbor kids were close to our boys' ages, so they would come over and play—Jake, Sissy, and Shannon. What fun times those five little kids had.

Then a young deaf girl named Lisa was added to the mix. She was able to communicate enough that they could play together. We added an aboveground swimming pool, which became a playground for the kids as they got a bit older. In the winter our steep hill made for great sledding on those round discs. You just had to be careful not to end up out in the road. We had many big trees so there were always lots of leaves to make into piles in the fall—great for jumping into. It was a wonderful place to raise kids.

One year, we had a bad flood and the Susquehanna River covered much of Wilkes-Barre. Gene was stuck across the river manning a water facility to keep it running, while the boys and I were at home up on the mountain. It was a frightening time, and we all missed him greatly. After about four days, he was finally able to get back across to us. He got lots of hugs and kisses, I must say!

As the boys grew into toddlers, and Gene had finished all his education, I decided to return to work but not to floor nursing. I had my heart set on becoming a nurse anesthetist, so I spent a year studying my chemistry, anatomy, physiology, and pharmacy drug textbooks before applying for anesthesia school. It was *not* delightful and stimulating reading, but I wanted to be sharp on the subjects, as it had been eleven years since I graduated from nursing school.

In 1974 when the boys were two and three years old, I went to school at Wilkes-Barre School of Anesthesia at Wilkes-Barre General Hospital. To make it possible for me to go back to school, we had to find daycare for the boys. In unbelievable timing, a church opened up a child-care center a couple miles away from us, right at the start of my schooling. Since I had to leave for work so early, Gene fed the boys, dressed them, and took them to daycare before work. That worked out well for many reasons, but mostly because he could impart to them a happy mood to start the day—he's a morning person. I'm a night person and don't like to even talk before 10 a.m., so the boys were much better off starting the days with their dad.

The daycare staff took great care of our boys; one of the ladies even took them home with her if we were unable to get back up the mountain before the center closed for the day.

Right after I graduated, the daycare closed. The boys were then old enough to go to school. Talk about God's provision and timing!

The hospital had just started the anesthesia program and I was in the second class—one of only two students, so we got lots of experience in cases. That was back in the era when we still scrubbed out the endotracheal tubes, sterilized them, and used them again.

Nowadays, we have single-use endotracheal tubes wrapped in sterile packaging, which are much safer to use, offer less chance of infections, and eliminate the chance of transferring diseases from one patient to the next. (Plus, it eliminated the need to scrub out and hand-sterilize the tubes!) We cleaned a lot of supplies, restocked carts, and learned all the techniques used in administering anesthesia. As part of our training, we learned the science behind drugs and interactions with the body; we learned the way to determine dosages of drugs for patients; we learned how to titrate the drugs until you got the effect you wanted; and how to constantly monitor the patients' level or depth of sleep to keep them from having pain, make sure their muscles were relaxed, and keep them from waking up during the surgery.

As we practiced under the watchful eyes of our supervising instructors, we learned and became proficient in how to do it on our own. It was like an art form, in which you became more proficient the more you did it. During the two years, we learned the basics and then advanced to harder and more complicated cases to develop our skills. An instructor or anesthesiologist always stood close at hand to watch over us and answer questions. At the end of the two years, we took a state board test, which I passed to become a certified registered nurse anesthetist (CRNA).

I was where I was meant to be—I liked having the responsibility of keeping a patient safe under the anesthesia, and then making sure they woke up in a comfortable state. The more times I took a patient to the recovery room awake, not having pain, and responsive to the recovery room nurses, the better I felt about giving anesthesia. I will admit, it is a stressful field at times, as things can go along so smoothly, and then in an instant, become critical. "Hours of boredom and moments of sheer panic" is how some people describe anesthesiology.

Chapter 2

Sometimes during our schooling, we had to take patients to the recovery room and put them on a ventilator until the effects of the drugs/gases wore off and they woke up. In addition to learning the science, we had to learn the *art* of doing the dance of timing; and create enough relaxation of the patient's muscles and abdominal cavity so the surgeon could operate easily; and keep the patient asleep enough so they didn't know or feel anything. That was just in surgery. Then we had to know how to wake them, extubate them, and take them to recovery room, being sure the patients could respond and control their breathing. Sounds easy, right? Trust me, it's an *art* and balancing act.

We also had to consider the health histories and issues of each patient, which added another layer of concerns to deal with and watch. We had to know the chemistry and dosages of the drugs and gases, and how to balance them all, along with keeping the patients hydrated enough to balance out any blood loss. Can you say *balancing act*?

I was so motivated to do well in anesthesia that I passed all my tests with flying colors. These studies were serious business—no partying or having all the fun experiences I'd had in nursing school.

Have you ever had to do something difficult and exacting—where someone's life was depending on your skill? Well, there were many times I faced difficult intubations and needed to quickly get that tube down the trachea to give the patient oxygen and gases for the surgery. Talk about stress! I learned to block out all the distractions around me and hone in on the job right in front of me. It was a much-needed skill—not only then but in other situations in life.

Maybe you find yourself in a demanding job or life situation and are feeling the stress weighing heavily on you and even impacting your physical health. It's time to find a way to learn how to deal with those stressors, lessen them, or change circumstances.

Hone in on the important things and block out the others. We all have stress in one form or another but we all react differently. Maybe it's as simple as an attitude adjustment so that stress doesn't have a stranglehold and tie you in knots. Learn to let things slide off your back. Ask yourself: how important will this be in five minutes, five hours, five days, five months? If it's not much—don't let it have so much importance now.

I graduated in 1976 and became a CRNA—certified registered nurse anesthetist—which enabled me to also become an ARNP—advanced registered nurse practitioner. I was getting almost as many letters after my name as Gene was with his four degrees! RN, CRNA, ARNP, and later I got CNHP—Certified Natural Health Professional. Whoo-hoo—that made it look like I really knew something!

We both worked for several years in Pennsylvania until we moved to Tarpon Springs, Florida, in 1978, where Gene took a job as general manager of West Coast Regional Water Supply Authority. He was there twelve years before moving to another job.

We loved living in Florida, as it was so much warmer than the cold winters in the mountains of Pennsylvania. No more icy roads with the snow coming down so heavily you could hardly see, or fog so thick that visibility was almost nil. I can remember driving back home up the mountain one time able to see only the white line at the side of the road for guidance. Scary.

When we moved to Florida, I began working at Morton Plant Hospital in Clearwater in the anesthesia/surgery department, but after seven years of long one-hour commutes, I decided to work closer to home. I'd had enough of driving in heavy traffic, and wanted to be closer to home with the boys in school.

In 1985 I went to work at St. Luke's Eye Clinic in Tarpon Springs and worked there for six and a half years, doing eye blocks and monitoring cases in surgery. The job was a whole new way of utilizing my anesthesia training. One of the scariest things I've ever done was learning how to do injections alongside the eye to make it numb and immobile for cataract surgery. Two physician's assistants performed eye blocks as well, just to keep all the patients ready for Dr. Gills. At times I asked them to help me finish an eye block because I was scared to death I would hurt the patients and their eyes. It was several months before I felt confident and capable in doing the blocks and able to be a productive member of the team. I would prepare the patients with their injections and then put a pinky ball on to lower the eye pressure before the procedure. This was back in the old days when we used a pink rubber ball with a strap attached to it. After numbing the eye, we put the ball on the eye and then wrapped the strap around the head to keep compression on the eye so the eye pressure would decrease. That made it safer to open the eye to remove the cataract. Close to the end of my time working there, they developed a new technique of numbing the eyes with eye drops. It was so much easier on us—and the patients.

Still, I felt I was losing my general surgery anesthesia skills doing only locals at the eye clinic, so in 1991 I went to work with Pinellas Anesthesia Associates at Helen Ellis Hospital in Tarpon Springs. We administered anesthesia all over the hospital—in the operating rooms; for outpatient surgery; in the x-ray department; in the cardiac cath lab; in OB for deliveries; in the endo department for colonoscopies, EGDs, and ERCPs; and even out in trucks with lithotripsy machines to break up kidney stones.

At times we also were assigned to different surgery centers to work for the day. I often drove to New Port Richey, Countryside, Belleair, two centers in Tampa, as well as the surgicenter in the hospital. All the diversity of different locations kept the work interesting.

In 2005 I decided to become an independent contractor to have more control over my working time. I went down to four, and then three days a week of work. I still worked for Pinellas Anesthesia Associates and would go where they sent me. I worked for a total of nineteen years at Helen Ellis Hospital and the free-standing surgery centers that we covered for anesthesia services.

When we first moved to Tarpon Springs, I went to work at Morton Plant Hospital but also discovered an opportunity for additional income. I was introduced to Mary Kay Cosmetics through a friend. After joining the company, I set a goal to become a director, and achieved it in six months. I enjoyed teaching skin care classes, attending the meetings, going to conventions, and having to get *way* out of my comfort zone to speak to large groups of people. That was a catalyst to help me grow out of my shyness, which developed after I chipped my teeth as a child, resulting also in a scar and a slight lisp. So getting involved in Mary Kay made me feel more comfortable talking with people.

After being a director for about a year, I decided that was not what I really wanted to do in life. The jewelry, cars, and awards weren't what I needed or wanted. What really brought me satisfaction was to help people—to serve them in some way. So I left that endeavor and just focused on working in anesthesia.

Life Outside of Work

One year after moving to Tarpon Springs, my husband bought me a horse for my birthday. I have always loved horses—as most young girls do—but never thought I'd have one. "Lady," a seventeen-year-old quarter horse, became my pride and joy. She was nothing fancy, but she was *my* horse. I learned how to take care of her and soon realized how expensive it was to pay for feed, hay, medicines, riding gear, and vet services.

Chapter 2

We were fortunate to live near a barn where they boarded horses, so I kept Lady there at night and at our home during the day. We had a fenced field behind our house where she was able to graze. Gene built a three-sided little barn so she had a sun and rain shelter. I put a rope across our driveway so she couldn't get out but could roam all over our yard and eat grass. To scratch her belly, she would walk over small trees or bushes and rub back and forth. When I yelled at her to stop, she would run off, then stop and blow raspberries at me. I think she had a sense of humor.

Each morning I rode Lady bareback to our house as she trotted home for her food. One morning I slept in, so I was late getting to the barn to bring her home to be fed. On our way to the house, she decided to stop suddenly to eat grass, and I rode up her backbone and broke my tailbone. Talk about pain upon sitting! I had to sit on a donut for an extended time before things healed. Plane trips were excruciating because I couldn't easily get up and walk about and had to endure sitting on this sore area for the entire trip.

I had Lady to ride and love until she was twenty-nine. She developed a cough, so the vet put her on steroids, which she was on for six years. The medicine caused her adrenals to shrink and she became skinny and had no energy. One day when I was out in the garage, she walked over to me and laid her head on my shoulder, as if to say, "I can't go on—I've had enough. Please let me go to sleep." I called the vet and he came to put her down.

That was one of the saddest days of my life, losing a friend who would let me cry on her, hug her, and ride on her back up and down the roads and in the woods. I still, after all these years, get choked up when I think of Lady and how I loved her.

Horses are special animals to me, but we also had our share of dogs and cats, a big white rabbit, and a ferret. If you've ever had animals, you know how much love and fun they can add to your life. Their love is unconditional and freely given. All they want is for you to feed them, and give them love and attention.

We had a dog, Tippy, that was extremely shy when we first adopted him from the SPCA. He was covered in fleas and scared of his own shadow. After a period of time with all our love and attention, he blossomed into a real social butterfly—sorry—*dog*. He would visit all around the neighborhood, or even go to town for all we knew. He would then leave for months until we were convinced he was dead and decided to get another dog. Suddenly, he would show up looking the worse for wear, even sporting bad wounds. We'd take care of him, feed him, and love on him, and then he'd take off again. We figured he had a lady love somewhere far off. Eventually he didn't return home, so we got two dogs to replace him.

Our boys were busy in sports—first soccer and then football. Gene spent eight years coaching and taking them to practices and games. Sports have never been an interest in my life, so I only enjoyed going to games when they were playing. But if our boys were involved, I'd be there.

Many of their friends came to our house often to play ball with the boys out in our field. The sounds of grunts from tackles, yells of encouragement to teammates, or just good-natured ribbing of each other—all made us happy to have all the kids at the house, so we knew where they were and what they were doing. My grocery bills in those days seemed to take half my paycheck!

One year at Easter time, we hid colored plastic eggs all over the yard and out in the field and let these teenage boys and girlfriends have an Easter egg hunt. They still remember that and talk about all the fun they had.

If you have kids, you know about all the time, effort, and love you pour into their lives to let them know you love them, are interested in their lives, and care about how they turn out as adults.

Our efforts and sacrifices are never wasted, as they impact our kids for the rest of their lives. Then you can experience the joy as they follow your example to impact their own kids.

Our sons both did well in high school, graduating in 1988 and '89. Brent went to Clemson for his first year of college, but didn't like being so far from home. He then transferred to the University of Florida in Gainesville for the rest of his college years. Kurt followed him, and they shared an apartment with other boys. Talk about making a grown man cry—Gene and I both cried when our first son drove off in his truck to go to college! Our time with them was ending and it didn't feel good. We missed them being home. They kept things hopping with all their sports, activities, and friends.

Gene is an environmental engineer and is often active with his job. He is in management and has degrees in marketing and finance. The boys loved what he did, so they followed in his footsteps. It took them each five and a half years to graduate, but they now are independent contractors and have formed their own environmental engineering company together. They work with several counties in Florida and are project managers of various jobs.

Both of our sons are married and have brought daughters-in-love into our lives, as well as grandsons and step-granddaughters. One thing I never had was grandparents to impact my life with their presence, knowledge, and love. So Gene and I decided to be very present in our grandkids' lives. We determined they would know we love them, and we would pour our experiences and knowledge into them. They live close by, so we share wonderful family ties and a strong bond of love. We have even all traveled together on two family vacations out west where we created memories that will last long after Gene and I are gone.

Stage Two to a Meaningful Final Quarter: *Purpose*

The second stage toward creating a meaningful fourth quarter begins earlier in life, often revealed in the first quarter and further defined in the second quarter of life—*purpose*. The purpose God made clear to me in my second quarter was that I was to love and serve people. Your purpose will help you determine which direction to take in life and the choices that will lead you there. Your purpose will give you the ambition, aspiration, and inspiration to move toward your destiny in spite of any challenges along the way. The purpose of your life will also create in you the principles by which you operate and live.

In 1992, something began to happen to me. I exhibited several symptoms that made my life seem dark and dreary. I was full of emotional distress and began to feel as though I had no purpose for living. I couldn't control my responses when Gene spoke to me, so he avoided me to protect himself from my sharp tongue. The more he steered clear of me, the more upset I felt inside.

I didn't like myself and no one else liked me at the time either. My monthly periods stopped, I started having crying jags, and one night I lay awake planning how to leave home. I even figured out where to go, what I could take with me, how I could support myself, how I'd get around, and how I would hide from everyone. I even contemplated suicide. I didn't know what was wrong, but I did not feel like myself. For a whole year I struggled with these symptoms and feelings.

During this time, I turned fifty, but my friends were afraid to give me any gag gifts because I was in such a precarious emotional state. They couldn't be sure how I would react. A year or so later, my good friend Roberta gave me a walker with wheels on it so I could still go Rollerblading in my advancing years! I was finally able to laugh then and appreciate her sense of humor. Rollerblading was something I loved doing, as I could fly down the trail, dancing to the music I listened to on my headset, and enjoying the freedom of movement. For a year or two, I would go three to four times a week on the Pinellas Trail on a thirteen-mile circuit and really stayed in shape. As life took over, I went less and less, until I was lucky to go Rollerblading once or twice a week.

During this time, one day at work the anesthesiologist had to put the patients to sleep for me because I couldn't stop crying. It would not inspire much confidence in the patient that I could do my job if they saw me weeping during their procedure. The surgery supervisor finally pulled me aside and asked why I was crying.

"I have no idea!" I exclaimed.

"How old are you?" she asked.

"Forty-nine."

"Honey, you are probably in menopause."

Menopause? Could that really be it? Could all the drama and changes I had been experiencing come down to hormones? She sent me to a lady gynecologist who examined me and tested my hormone levels. Sure enough, I had been going into menopause. The doctor prescribed a hormone regimen, and after three days, I was back to normal. I couldn't believe that I'd been unable to recognize what was happening to me, but I was too close to the situation. I thought I was too young for menopause since my male gynecologist had said I was.

What a year of hell that was—not only for me but everyone around me, especially my family. It certainly gave me an appreciation for what some women go through with the changes that take place when menopause sets in. This was in and of itself a *defining moment*, as it changed my mind-set about women.

Through these struggles and the emotional roller-coaster ride, I developed a profound appreciation for women that I had not had before. Prior to going through my own year of personal hell, I had thought many women were catty, jealous, and vindictive. And remember, I had few fond memories of girls growing up and had wanted sons, not daughters. As an adult, I had no real, close relationships with other women. But after going through my own personal crisis, I found that women show strength to endure things that men have not had to go through, and come through on the other side as more empathetic, compassionate, and loving to other women who are struggling with the same things. There is a sisterhood in what women must deal with.

I became open to relationships, friendships, and all the sustaining support women could bring into my life. It was like the opening of a flower with a light fragrance, an unfolding beauty that was a joy to behold.

I started looking at them with eyes of love and have developed enduring friendships with a number of women. We may not see each other for years, but can pick right up where we left off when we get together again. That connection is sustained through trials, aging, time, and distance. It's a beautiful thing. Up to this time, I knew I loved my sisters, but we didn't have a really close bond. After going through this struggle, I became more open to sharing and relating to them in a real and deeper way. We have come to value our bonds and try to vacation together at least once every year or two. We include our husbands, as they know they would be missing out on so much fun if they didn't come along.

Chapter 2

I have come to think women are stronger than we are given credit for. As we go through life, we search for the right man, and for some it ends up being a lifelong search. We must also become the right woman for some man, and that takes a lifetime! We bear the children; take care of the house; shop and prepare meals; and act as chauffeur, nurse, manager of monies, scheduler of appointments, teacher, and lover and friend to our husband. We are the disciplinarian, seamstress, painter, baker, and dietician. We often work at outside jobs and seek fulfillment with the skills and experience we've gained. And we look good doing it all. Just considering women in and of themselves gives me a greater appreciation for their strengths.

I am not knocking men; we need them to balance us in our God-given functions, needs, and desires for love and life. We complete each other by contributing our strengths as well as our weaknesses to his. We bring our love, abilities, and gifts to the marriage table to add to the whole.

Marriage is almost like learning to dance. For a while one leads and the other follows; then circumstances may change, and the follower must take over leading for a while. This shift can be a thing of beauty—or disturbing, distasteful, tough to change, embarrassing to not be able to lead, hard to let go of traditional roles. But it can also be freeing to no longer be forced to carry the load alone. This may allow the other partner to do what is necessary for that season of time.

I have changed so much through our years of marriage. I came to it shy, uncertain of who I was or what I could do. Even though I had achieved academically, I was stunted emotionally and had a lot of growing to do. Things I experienced as a young girl had impacted me badly and I had a hard time trusting. It has taken years to come out of my protective shell. Gene has had a lot to deal with as I have gone through my struggles and growth. I love him for allowing me the freedom to endure and fight through my issues to emerge from my cocoon and become a beautiful butterfly, now able to spread my wings and fly.

Have you experienced great struggles in your marriage, in learning to adapt and live 24/7 with another person, in wondering if the pain and work of birthing a strong union is worth it all? Have you found yourself ready to throw in the towel and say, "I'm out of here. I can't take this situation anymore"? I understand, as Gene and I have been there several times. "But God . . ." is the only reason we have managed to let go of the *divorce* word and decide to carry on. God is the one who gave me this verse to hang my hat on:

Create in me a clean heart, O God, and renew a right spirit within me. Cast me not away from thy presence and take not thy Holy Spirit from me.
—Psalm 51:10 KJV

I sang that verse over and over to God during the difficult times until my heart finally *did* change. It wasn't overnight by any means, but it was the starting point for growth, a change of heart, mind, and soul. Because I persevered through the storms and struggles, our marriage is stronger and deeper now. If you are experiencing similar troubles, all I can tell you is to make God your strong and solid foundation and hang in there. Depend on Him for your strength and to make you a new creation. He will do it—He did it for me!

I'm not saying that if you are yoked with another person you won't still have to deal with differences in personalities, desires, and focus. Gene and I still do, but now we are pulling more in unity to achieve our goals and purpose in life. I'm still a night person; he's still a morning sunshine person. We are still different, but we're not fighting each other as much anymore. It makes me think of the words "iron sharpens iron," and I have to think we have helped smooth the rough edges off each other.

There is mutual benefit in the rubbing of two iron blades together; the edges become sharper, making the knives more efficient in their task to cut and slice.
—Howard Hendricks

As iron sharpens iron, so one person sharpens another.
—Proverbs 27:17

How are your edges? Are you allowing your spouse or close friend to admonish, correct, criticize, or lovingly share areas that need to be improved upon in your life? Do you accept such correction and take it to heart, or fling it back in your loved one's face as your hurt, rage, and frustration boil over with angry words? Sometimes it takes time to let God do the changing work in us, because we can try all we want on our own, but if it isn't happening in our heart, it's not going to last. Hang in there, things can get better in the second quarter.

I speak to this from the vantage point of being many years past our times of turmoil. Let me share with you more of our years of just living life, as our boys grew up, left home, and experienced more defining moments to help channel the direction my life was taking as the third quarter began.

The Third Quarter

Ages 51–75

The third quarter of life is a time of maturing and *refining* for many as we finish up our working careers and either enter full-blown retirement or find our dreams and passions, dust them off, and put them into gear now that we have more time and financial freedom to do so. It may be a time of traveling to exotic places around the world, or spending more time at home with family. It can become a time of more interaction with a new set of friends and business interests; a time of learning more tech-y things; a time of writing memoirs or books; a time to spend on hobbies; or a time to build wealth or monies to retire on, pay off mortgages, buy that retirement home, or the "toys" we have always wanted, e.g. car, boat, RV, etc.

The third quarter can also be a time of health issues coming to the forefront and limiting our abilities to do as much as we used to. Our health choices start way back in the first quarter, which can set the stage for our health situation now, for better or worse.

Chapter 3

Third Quarter—The Refining
1993–2018

As the years went by, Gene and I stayed busy living our lives—working full-time, taking care of our sons, and attending games as the boys played soccer and football all through school. I taught Bible studies for eighteen years and led women's groups in our church, and Gene and I both sang in the choir. Our lives were full.

Back in 1978 when we moved from Pennsylvania to Florida, we found a great church and had attended there for twenty-seven years. We shared life with our church family—going camping; enjoying meals together; attending retreats; studying the Bible; singing in choir; and sharing concerns, joys, and grief.

Our choir group was our "living life together" family, and the joys we experienced presenting cantatas and drama musicals at Easter and Christmas really brought us together. A group of us went to Brooklyn, New York, for a choir workshop led by the 250-member Brooklyn Tabernacle Choir. Their choir members came from every walk of life, but they had allowed God to change and reshape their lives, so when they sang, it was with their whole hearts. They had no sheet music; they learned by hearing and practicing their parts by sections: alto, soprano, tenor, and bass. Then they put it all together.

We were able to practice and then sing with them—a once-in-a-lifetime experience. Have you ever been on stage and sung with over six hundred people from choirs all over the nation? Oh, the sound of praise we made. It made the floor and walls vibrate! I still get goose bumps at the memory of those songs we sang together.

Over the years, we had several different pastors and we adjusted to each one's different style. Then a new pastor came who changed things drastically when he did away with our choir, orchestra, and handbell choir and changed the worship leadership to a praise team. All these decisions were so the church would be more in tune with current times and appeal to a younger age group.

Gene and I tried to adjust to all the changes and find our niche, but our once-comfortable church now felt uncomfortable and almost foreign. Over time we felt like we were no longer a part of the body or even needed. The focus became reaching young families with children. The vision of the church had shifted. And while it wasn't a deliberate snub of the older members, we felt as if we had served our time and now needed to make way for the younger generation—as if being older made us irrelevant. So Gene and I quietly left, as did many others. We left friends and "family" who had been our support and comfort in times of need, and as a result, felt adrift. It was *so* painful, *so* lonely, *so* depressing. It was like going through a divorce—being torn from a life partner.

Looking back, I can see how God used this situation to take us out of our comfort zone to remind us that we have nothing to rely on except Him, and that we needed to develop our own personal relationship with Him as our anchor, support, strong tower, and friend. Being active in church was not to be a replacement for a personal relationship with Him.

Maybe you have gone through a traumatic time in your life, where things were great for a while, and then turned into a seeming nightmare. Your life turned upside down and nothing was the same.

You didn't know if you could go on, or wondered if life would ever be worth living again. I think God allows us to experience situations where our backs are against the wall and nothing the world offers helps us, where our only option is to turn to Him and ask Him to lift us up out of that deep, dark pit and set our feet on solid ground again.

The Lord is my rock and my fortress and my deliverer, my God is my rock, in whom I take refuge, my shield, and the horn of my salvation, my stronghold.
—Psalm 18:2

That's not such a bad place to be, as it can turn us back in the right direction again. It did that for Gene and me.

≈≈≈

Stage Three to a Meaningful Final Quarter: *Presents (or Gifts/Talents)*

The third stage of creating lasting meaning in life is to define the presents or gifts God gives us in our lives. I never knew that simply reading a magazine article would bring an extraordinary present/gift that would lead to a complete change in our lives and future, and would take my life's purpose to another level.

Our presents are not to be hoarded or used only to satisfy our own egos or for selfish gain. They are given to us so we can in turn offer them to others. The presents/gifts you have will help define your contribution to society and your legacy. They are an offering given to us to then be used for or given to others.

An "Essential" Moment

Around that period in our lives, I experienced what would be another *defining moment* in my life—the day I was introduced to essential oils. I can say it so calmly and quietly, but the impact it brought to our lives was almost earth-shaking. Little did I know that these oils would play an integral part in redefining my life's purpose.

In 1997 I was simply reading an article, being present at that moment to receive information that would change our lives. The article, "Nature's Amazing Healing Oils" in *BioTech News*, introduced a company called Young Living Essential Oils. They produced oils from plants that were helpful for health issues, giving support for every body system, and other benefits. The article explained the chemical properties of the oils and their effects on the body, how to use them, and what they could do in the body, and included testimonials from doctors and people who had experienced the health benefits of essential oils for themselves.

Reading this article was a *defining moment* in my life because I felt the strong nudge to order these oils and experience the effects for myself. They so helped me that I stopped all OTC meds. I felt better and had more energy. And others started to notice. People would catch a whiff of the oils on me and ask about them, so I shared what I had experienced in getting rid of headaches, tight muscles, digestive issues, sleep issues, as well as hormone problems, and told them how to get them for themselves at wholesale cost. I was not out to make money. I truly wanted to help people by sharing what had helped me. After all, that's what I did as a nurse—care for others.

The essential oils became a big part of my life. I used them all the time, but my husband was skeptical about this "woo-woo" stuff. When he finally went to the company's convention with me several years later, he heard from scientists and doctors about the valid scientific explanations for the oils' healthy effects. He then became a user himself, and someone who appreciated their impact on health issues. He even brought people to me or told them to come to me to receive help for their specific issue.

We were at a picnic on a lake one time when a young lady inadvertently stepped into an ant's nest. She got ant bites all over her feet and was panicking because she was highly allergic to their venom. She knew she'd be having problems soon. She came to me because Gene told her I could help her. I ran and got my oils and put lavender, Thieves (a Young Living blend for infection), and peppermint all over her feet and legs. I had her smell the lavender to help her calm down, and soon she was much improved. Since she didn't have her Benadryl with her, she would have had to go to the ER to deal with the problem, but the oils helped calm down her emotions and her allergic reaction. Scenarios like this are why I carry my oils everywhere I go—I can't imagine being without them.

Gene and I both have our own stashes on our bathroom counters, and the oils keep us functioning in health and make our skin more youthful looking.. He comes into my office to look up what oils to use for his specific issue, and then gets them out of my supplies. He went from being a skeptic to a believer—I loved it!

One health problem Gene struggled with for over ten years was rosacea. After using essential oils, he wrote this testimony for me, and another testimony about a second health issue:

Rosacea: A Skin Problem That Just Keeps Getting Worse

It has been over ten years that I've observed this condition on my face. It started with inflammations on my nose in the first years, which were generally temporary. I treated this initially with a topical corticosteroid with fairly good results. Then the inflammations became more frequent and begin on my cheeks, then just above my eyebrows, then on the temples and forehead. I found that topical corticosteroid (which isn't supposed to be used over a long term) was losing its effectiveness and the inflammation areas were becoming more severe with deeper skin involvement and more severe associated infections. I tried other products on the market for rosacea with little success.

A year ago, I started to experiment with Young Living oils. After some early trials I found a combination that worked beyond my wildest dreams. I use three oils: ylang-ylang, cypress, and frankincense. These oils are applied by fingertip to the areas that have a history of inflammation. The oils are rotated one in the morning, the second in the evening, and the third the next morning. The cycle simply continues thereafter morning and evening. I apply a healing moisturizer (I have had good success with Jergens) after the oils.

After a couple of weeks of this procedure, I noticed significant improvement in my skin health. As time has passed, my skin is generally without blemish. The rosacea is still lurking about, but the inflammations when they occur are minor and heal within a couple of days instead of weeks. Overall, I now look in the mirror when I get up in the morning without fear of what new inflammation I will see on my face. Sooooo thankful.

Prostate: An Elevated PSA Is a Concern

Oh joy, another issue to worry about. Yes, my annual PSA came back elevated, and the statistics I read shows a correlation between an elevated PSA and prostate cancer. Having overcome my skepticism with oils and their effectiveness in the treatment of rosacea, I decided to try the oils on the prostate issue. Checking the *Reference Guide to Essential Oils*, I found some suggestions of oils that have shown effectiveness for prostate health. So I decided to try a one-month application of a combination of the suggested oils: frankincense, myrrh, fennel, and ImmuPower [a Young Living blend for supporting the immune system.] I used the vegi-capsules and added two drops of each of the four oils as a suppository morning and night for one week. I used a carrier oil for the suppository lubricant.

For the next three weeks I rotated the four oils—one oil at a time using four drops—morning and night. Then it was time for another PSA test. The reading had dropped back to the normal range. Again, I was delighted to receive the benefits of essential oils.

Gene Heath, 12/3/14

Many women who use essential oils have issues with husbands who are cynical about the oils having such profound effects, and these women must tolerate down-putting remarks. It may take years for men to try the oils for themselves and appreciate how they can help. So if your husband is like that, don't give up—just give him time. When he has a need, he'll ask for an oil to try. I heard the story of a woman whose husband hated the smell of oils and told her not to use them in the house. So she started using Joy (a Young Living blend for dealing with blocks to being loved in our lives) in his underwear drawer to lightly scent his boxers. One day, weeks later, he came home early while she was ironing and diffusing Joy.

He said it really smelled good in the house and asked what it was. When she told him, he said she could use that oil because he liked it. So, try them slowly and watch for positive results with your husband over time.

As we were returning from convention in 2013, flying home with our heads full of new information we had learned, Gene turned to me and said, "Okay, what do you want to do now?"

I knew he meant "What do you want to do with your business?" so without hesitation I answered, "Teach."

"Then go for it," he said.

I started creating classes on essential oils and teaching those who wanted to learn about this new way to deal with health issues. I was learning along with them as we studied the many ways the oils helped, how to use them, as well as how to make recipes for different home uses. It was an exciting time watching people open up to using something other than drugs all the time, and actually experiencing results with essential oils.

I was still working as an independent contractor nurse anesthetist covering vacations for other CRNAs. As I got busier teaching classes and then conducting tours to teach my team members in Indiana, Illinois, and Georgia, I was less and less available when needed for coverage. I remember a number of phone calls like this:

> "Sue, can you come in tomorrow to cover for so and so?"
> "Well, I don't think I can get there in time, as I am in Georgia (or Illinois, or Indiana)."

Chapter 3

So in September 2014, I officially retired from administering anesthesia. I was just too busy teaching and traveling, and going on mission trips.

Unfortunately, it wasn't until I was fifty-four that I learned about essential oils and how they were a great help with emotions, hormones, and all the PMS emotions. I learned it about four years too late for myself, but it was "better late than never" in finding out how important they were for our lives and health. I was also eager to share with other women the benefits of these oils during the menopausal years, so they'd have a less traumatic experience than I had. If I'd learned about the oils earlier, I feel like I could have helped my horse with her respiratory issues and myself with menopause—and all with less trauma.

Trish is a friend I've taught about essential oils, and she now uses them in her classroom where she teaches. She diffuses Thieves to counteract all the germs that kids bring to school and helps to keep the kids healthier in her classroom. She told me of a recent occurrence when essential oils literally saved her life.

Trish and her husband were preparing for a hurricane that was threatening Florida with a category 5 storm. They decided to use their garage as their safe room, so she went to put the garage door down. When it wouldn't go down smoothly, she discovered a wasp nest in the doorjamb. They attacked her, stinging her all about her head and face. She used her cell phone to call her husband, who was on an upper floor, telling him to bring her oils down. She took Purification (a Young Living blend for antiseptic, antibacterial, antifungal, and sanitizing effects) and started pouring it all over her head to neutralize the venom from the stings. She rubbed it in, and added lavender oil to help with the pain.

Soon her face was extremely swollen, and she could hardly move her lips to speak. She began to lose her vision and she was sweating profusely; she felt like she was going to lose consciousness. She continued to use the oils with her husband's help. He ran next door to see if the neighbor had any Benadryl, but she only had a cold tablet. Trish took one even though she wasn't sure it had much or any Benadryl in it.

About forty-five minutes later, Trish began to return to normal. She said later that she knew the oils were the only thing that saved her, as she was very close to "going out." She and her husband now have a greater appreciation of the power of the oils to help even in a life-threatening situation.

One of my friends, Lisa, owns horses and uses essential oils on them to deal with sore muscles, wounds, and belly aches from colic. She asked me to do a Raindrop Technique (a series of specific oils and movements to help enhance health) on her horse, Walker. He's eighteen-and-a-half hands high—kinda big—so I had to stand on a stepstool to reach his back. He loved the smell, all the rubbing, and the impact of the oils. After I was finished, I gave him a packet of Ningxia Red, a healthy anti-oxidant drink by Young Living, and he couldn't get enough of it. He kept licking the bowl, trying to find another drop he might have missed. Lisa used the oils on him daily, and gave him Ningxia Red to keep him healthy. She also had a dog with mast cell tumors on her leg, as well as glaucoma. She utilized the oils extensively and felt they gave her more years of life with her dog.

Lisa's husband burned his hand badly when he picked up a hot iron skillet without a glove. She put lavender on it several times to alleviate the blistering, redness, and pain. The next morning, he was amazed that his hand looked as though it had never been burned. He is now a big believer. When preparing to sell their home, she used Thieves cleaner all throughout the house to clean it, sprayed it in the air conditioner vents to clean out the mold and mildew, and diffused it whenever possible buyers came to see the house. They remarked on how good her house smelled. Her house did sell to another horse lover, and she was able to share how the oils had helped her horses' health.

Young Living essential oils have become a natural part of our lives. We use them daily—morning and night—to keep us healthy and our immune systems high. Just ask me about a health issue and I'll say, "There's probably an oil for that!"

All in all, the start to my third quarter of life brought much change. Sons graduated and moved on, making their own lives. Gene and I experienced an empty nest. We dealt with leaving a church family we'd loved for decades and having to move on to a different place. But we also experienced the change to a more intimate relationship with God, and began to see how He was also changing and redirecting our purpose in life. Learning about and then experiencing the benefits of essential oils had an effect not just on our friends and us but on many others. I was about to see how God would use them to bring about an even greater purpose in my life.

Have you experienced challenges and changes in your life too? Have they shaken up your stability, beliefs, direction, and purpose in life? I don't know about you, but after looking back, I can see that we needed that shaking and changing to more finely tune the direction we were headed. Can you acknowledge that even though we don't like them, changes can be good at many points in our lives? We can so easily become stagnant running in the same rut, and if we want vibrant, "full of joy" lives, change is part and parcel of bringing it about.

Chapter 4
Early Dreams and New Passions

Remember my childhood dream of being a nurse or missionary? Well, obviously I had pursued the dream of nursing most of my life. That dream was not only fulfilled but had brought much joy and satisfaction to me through the years. Now both parts of my dream were about to join together, and it would change my life.

Stage Four to a Meaningful Final Quarter: *Place*

Another stage in creating a fulfilling and meaningful final quarter is to discover your *place*. Place is about geography, yes, but it's more than that. Place is the situation where your present/gift and your past experience and your passion come together to create an opportunity to accomplish the purpose God has set aside for you. I had not realized to this point that I was missing my ultimate sense of place. We had a wonderful life. I'd had a full, satisfying career and followed my dream of being a nurse. But ultimately, God had a specific place that would draw me to use my gifts and passions to help more people than I'd ever dreamed of.

What is your sense of place? It could be as small as your apartment, as big as your community, or as wide as the world. Your place may not be an actual location but a situation in your life or the lives of others. Do you feel you have discovered that, or are still on the way? Are you aware of the circumstances in your life that God might be using or arranging to bring you to your place?

After leaving our church home of twenty-seven years, we felt adrift. We visited several churches to search for a place that felt like home, where the Holy Spirit was alive and active in that place. We went to one church for at least five years, singing in the choir and participating in activities, but didn't join—we just felt leery of getting too attached. However, while we were there, the pastor announced a mission trip to the Amazon River to minister to small villages on the riverbank. The team would go for ten days and live on a boat traveling by night and tying up by day. They were looking for a nurse to join this trip.

Something nudged me in my spirit, and I turned to Gene and said, "We need to go on this!" We decided immediately to go together without hesitation. And this decision was a turning point in my life, as it ignited my love for missions . . . another *defining moment* as it brought me to my sense of *place*.

We flew into Manaus, Brazil, and then endured a long bus ride, a wait for a ferryboat to take us across the river, and then a bumpy van ride through the jungle to arrive in the village where we met the boat, our home for the next week and a half. As we exited the van,

Chapter 4

we were greeted by the sight and smell of many fish. Lots of big carts filled the street where fishermen unloaded their catch from the night before, including several different varieties of fish—even piranha! Lots of sharp teeth in those babies.

Just getting down to the boat was a trip in itself. We had to descend a lot of uneven and slippery wooden steps while carrying our hand luggage. Some of the native guys helped carry the big suitcases down on their heads. We were shocked to see electric lines hanging down in the water to connect the boats to electricity. The Amazon River can fluctuate thirty to fifty feet during the rainy season, so wires that might be out of water during the dry season are way under water when it rains. Something that dangerous would not be allowed in the United States, but it somehow looked normal in this setting. Life carried on there without mishap, at least none we encountered while on the river. These floating homes had little in the way of convenience, and we had expected primitive conditions. So we were amazed to find TVs on these flat riverboats—they had little else but were connected to the outside world through TV!

We finally made it to our boat and were shown to our rooms. They were compact spaces with bunk beds, and a shower with a big filter to strain out the grass and mud as the water came from the river. The room Gene and I had was right over the kitchen, which was down in the hold. We could smell the food being prepared and feel the heat that rose from the kitchen door. The food was delicious and nourishing, with lots of rice, some meat, and fruits and vegetables. We certainly didn't starve.

One time when we stopped for an overnight stay, we had to tie up next to the boat closest to the shore, so there was no docking room left for us, which made it a bit difficult to get to shore. Then we discovered that everyone on board that boat used the river as a bathroom, so Gene said he wasn't taking a shower with everything he knew was in the water. It was extremely *hot* and we were sweating like crazy, so I decided to be brave—or stupid—and just use the shower. I'm still here.

The doctor who arranged to go with us did not show up for our ten-day trip. Since we had no doctor, they put me in charge of the medical team. It was a *challenging and somewhat scary experience* since I'd had no previous exposure to tropical diseases. My medical team was comprised of me—a nurse anesthetist—and a veterinarian, home health nurse, and secretary. Thankfully, onboard the boat was a copy of the book *Village without a Doctor*, which I used every day to treat the health issues the people presented to us.

During our trip we stopped at three villages to minister to the people with a medical/dental clinic, and while there we also led vacation Bible school with the native kids.

Since we had a dentist with us, we were able to pull teeth for those who needed it. He required assistance to hold the patients' heads in place while he worked, so my husband volunteered. On the first day, as he watched the dentist administer the injections to numb the tooth, Gene started feeling queasy. When it took several tries to get a patient's wisdom tooth loose, Gene couldn't stand the sound of the grating on the tooth and fainted. It seemed to take forever to bring him back around, and all I could see in my mind's eye was having to keep his dead body on board in the heat for ten more days! Crazy, I know, but the mind does funny things when you are stressed. He finally came around, and we gently told him he should go help with vacation Bible school—outside and with the kids. He willingly accepted the verdict.

Chapter 4

Stage Five to a Meaningful Final Quarter: *Preparation*

The next stage toward filling your last quarter with meaning is *preparation*. It is not enough to know your gifts and see your path and place unfolding; you must be prepared to move forward into your purpose. Preparation is key to being effective in the pursuit of your dreams. When you are prepared, you are enabled to achieve the purpose on your path. This may require sacrifices in order to educate yourself. Take the time to learn and grow in areas of knowledge to become equipped for the work to come. I knew what I needed to learn when I returned from the Amazon, and that preparation gave me the tools to take the next steps. It also gave me a "rehearsal" of sorts before heading to a different mission location. Preparation laid a solid foundation for the work that was coming.

What preparation do you need to make in pursuit of your purpose right now? Where can you go or whom do you need to seek out in order to prepare?

I returned home with the knowledge that I needed to learn tropical diseases if I was going to go on more trips. The trip to the Amazon was another *defining moment* in my journey, because I discovered how much I didn't know. I did know that missions would be a part of my life from then on, and I also knew I was ready to prepare for where God was leading me. I was finally fulfilling the vision that was laid on my heart all those years ago as a young girl—to be a nurse/missionary! God had given me the desires of my heart.

> *Take delight in the LORD, and he will give you the desires of your heart.*
> —Psalm 37:4

After our trip, I began to research local medical professionals who might help me learn. I soon found a doctor from Largo, Florida, who taught a course on tropical diseases—Dr. Tonya Hawthorne. She founded New Frontiers Health Force, and is a medical missionary, having graduated from both Bible college and med school. She has taken mission teams to thirty countries to minister to people in all kinds of situations. While taking her course, I heard her describe the new direction she was taking her ministry—to concentrate on one country and set up a medical clinic, staff it with native medical personnel, supervise it for a number of years, and then move to set up another clinic somewhere else. She showed us a video of Kenya, her first location, and the village they had chosen for the clinic. The images of the children and people so tugged at my heart that I had tears rolling down my cheeks. I knew I had to go with her when she went—another *defining moment*. I had no idea how exactly, but everything up to this point, along with the new information I gained from Dr. Tonya's course, was preparing me for the place God was calling me to minister in missions.

My first trip with Dr. Tonya was in 2008 and presented a dangerous challenge. It was an election year in Kenya, and a government official's wife had been recently killed, so there was an uprising. Many people were shot and killed in the riots. The rebels set up roadblocks with big trucks across the highways, so no traffic could get into Nairobi. We were trying to get *out* of Nairobi to head

Chapter 4

for the village where we planned to work with and minister to the Masai people. It would be a good four-to-five-hour trip, as the roads were not paved most of the way.

As our team's van headed out to leave the city, we were enveloped in a massive traffic jam with everyone stopped. Men with rifles and shields surrounded the cars and our van. We could see jeeps of soldiers scattered throughout the traffic. We were cautioned not to take pictures, as the soldiers might seize our cameras. It's hard to describe the feelings I had, but it was as if we were in a bubble of God's protection, and amazingly the sight of all the guns did not terrify me.

After a while, two jeeps full of policemen pulled out of a police station to our left. Our van got in behind the first one, and the other jeep was in the rear. It was as if they'd arranged to escort us out of town! We drove through an intersection where tires were piled up and on fire. As we followed the jeep, it took us down a dirt road close to shops, homes, and outdoor markets and parallel to the main road. Finally, we got past the big trucks blocking the highway and drove down and over the grass divider to get up and onto the main road to head out of town. We made it safely to the village several hours later.

In those early years of our trips to Kenya, the roads were only paved a certain part of the way. The rest of the roads were potholed and rough, with rocks all over. We couldn't drive fast or the car would almost fall apart. Tire repair shops lined the streets just to handle all the damaged tires.

Today, the roads are paved all the way to Narok, the town nearest our village. The roads even extend several miles on out of that town. But then you hit the unpaved portion, and must slow down to about 10 mph. That section of the road is still horrendous, with washboard roughness, potholes, and rocks. Cars will drive all over the road to find the smoothest area. It's always a relief to finally reach our village, so our teeth can stop being jarred and we can stop breathing in dust. At times, some of our girls wear bandanas over their nose and mouth to cut down on the dust breathed in, and they look like bandits riding down the road.

One of the fun parts of riding on the roads out in the bush is seeing the wild animals off to the sides—zebras, giraffes, antelope of different varieties, dik-dik (the tiniest antelope), baboons, elephants, and many others. Sometimes they are fairly close, so you can get pictures. When we take a day to go out on safari we get great photos of the wildlife further off the roads—cheetahs, lions and lionesses, leopards, warthogs, hyenas, marmots, water buffalo, storks, and ostriches. Seeing these amazing animals in their natural habitat is breathtaking, but it's also a reminder of the danger they face. Our village is near the Masai Mara Reserve, 371,000 acres owned by the Masai people. Unfortunately, the reserve and its wildlife have been negatively impacted by tourism. Here's an excerpt from an article I found online about the Mara:

> Their show [of the animals migrating] is in danger of being upstaged. Every year, thousands upon thousands of tourists descend on the Masai Mara to witness the migration. The resident human population is increasing; lodges are proliferating. Rampant corruption means money is not filtering down to the Masai population, who are increasingly turning to charcoal and arable farming to make ends meet. In short, mankind is in danger of squandering one of the most important habitats left in the world.
>
> "It will not be long before it is gone, unless some drastic and urgent steps are taken now," says Joseph Ogutu, a scientist who has studied changes in the area's fauna for 24 years. The Masai Mara represents the northern quarter of the Serengeti ecosystem that stretches down into Tanzania. The wild

animals that remain here require vast and various dispersal areas to survive drought, predators and human pressure. These safe havens are disappearing. Lodges surrounding the park have erected kilometres of electric fencing; lions have been known to use them to trap their prey. . . .

The environment is displaying symptoms of its mismanagement. Algae are emerging in rivers upstream, a consequence of fertiliser use. The Mara River, where wildebeest cross from Tanzania, dried up completely in 2009, says Dickson Kaelo, a respected Masai guide. He recalls seeing scores of minibuses queueing to watch wildebeest splash through the water. But there was "just dust." Inside the treasured reserve, monkeys play with crisps packets. Even the predators' behavior is changing. Malaika is a cheetah who will sit on the roof of your car. . . .

Kenya's economy is heavily reliant on tourism, and the core area, the Mara National Reserve, generates an estimated £13m each year. The place projects a timelessness that speaks to notions of man's origins and the beginnings of time. But it also epitomizes a modern conflict over land and resources playing out across Africa today.[4]

As in so many other arenas, progress is not always a good thing.

Stage Six to a Meaningful Final Quarter: *Perseverance*

Once I had experienced Kenya, both the joys and the hardships of my first trip, I knew I had found my place. I also knew that *perseverance* would be key to continuing to serve there in the coming years, and I was dedicated to that commitment. I had to persevere in the work while I was there with the Masai, overcome the obstacles that are part of mission work, and prepare to help those who needed healing and wellness; I also had to have tenacity during all my time back at home in the States. It would be easy to just relax and enjoy being home, but I had to continue to learn, grow, and find the support I needed to return each time to Kenya.

What about your purpose requires you to persevere? Do you need to endure obstacles and struggles? Fear or lack of confidence? Do you have a steadfast faith in what God has called you to do? Let your passion for the purpose God has called you to follow help you persistently face whatever challenges await you.

On my first trip in 2008, I fell in love with the Masai people in Kenya. I knew I would return to minister through the clinic Dr. Tonya had started. In my second year at our village, I again took my oils, but I asked Dr. Tonya how God could use me, since I couldn't use my anesthesia skills and only had a few nursing skills that were needed, so what could I really do there with the oils I'd brought? How could I have any impact? She said to "just give it time and see what God does." I recall the situation now and see what a profound impact the oils have had in the clinic since then as people now come and ask just for oils to be applied. The essential oils have helped with many varied health-related situations even when I'm not there and are an integral part of what the clinic offers.

I've now gone to Kenya every year since 2008 using God's medicines—the essential oils—to minister to the people. I've been able to teach more than thirty people in the use and administration of the oils on patients that come to the medical clinic Dr. Tonya established, and that the Masai built in their village. The Masai people love the oils and their impact on physical needs. As a result, the oils' ministry has grown each year.

My company, Young Living Essential Oils, has graciously donated a hundred oils to the clinic each year to be used on the patients. This company has such a heart to minister to needs around the world and is willing to support the missionaries who go to countries that would not get the oils otherwise. The company goes to disaster areas—such as Nepal, where earthquakes and mudslides destroyed several villages—and helps the natives rebuild. To make bricks for their homes, Gary Young, the CEO and founder, sent two brick-making machines to the villages to enable the men to rebuild. They support several organizations worldwide that have ministries to suffering and needy people. I am blessed to have their interest and support in my endeavors. In 2015, I was honored at Young Living's Grand Convention with an Honorable Mention for the work I've been doing with the Masai.

I have countless stories of how the oils have ministered to the local people through the decade that I've been visiting Kenya and working with the Masai. So many people have captured my heart that I feel like I'm headed to my second home and my second family when I go each year. I miss them when I'm not there.

I spend most of my time working in the clinic, applying the oils on many of the patients as they come through, doing wound care, starting IVs, occasionally working in the pharmacy, teaching the clinic staff about the oils, sweeping floors, and loving on people. The following stories are only a tiny taste of the many lives changed in Kenya through the years I have been traveling there to help with the clinic. I am still amazed at the healing properties of the oils I am able to take and the way they minister to the Masai people.

The Final Quarter

One day in the clinic, Dr. Tonya brought a mother and her child to my room and said, "Sue, I want you to take care of her." The three-year-old little girl, Caroline, was badly burned all over her neck, right earlobe, and a portion of her shoulder. I asked Dr. Tonya, "Will you do the debriding?"

"No," she answered, "you take care of all of it."

I silently gulped because I had never had to debride a burn before. (Debriding is getting the dead skin off, so the fresh skin can grow underneath. It's a laborious process which can be uncomfortable, or even painful, for the patient.)

Beginning that day, I sprayed Lavaderm, a blend of lavender and aloe oils, to deal with the pain and moisten the burned tissue, then started the debriding. Caroline did not enjoy any of it, and neither did I. We had to hold her down to accomplish the job, and her mom, Diane, had tears in her eyes as she watched her little daughter endure this process. Every day Diane brought Caroline to the clinic and we started the procedure again. I made up a blend of healing oils to spray on after debriding, and as the weeks went by, we could see the healing taking place.

One day, Diane didn't make it in before the clinic closed for the day, so she and her daughter walked down the hill to our living compound. Caroline came running when she saw me and threw herself in my arms. I was blown away that she wasn't afraid of me and even trusted me to catch and hold her. We laughed and swung around just to celebrate seeing each other.

At the end of my time there that year, three and a half weeks later, Caroline's neck was healed—no infection, scars, or contractures. I was thrilled to see how the oils had benefited the whole healing process. The next year, I again saw Diane and Caroline in the clinic. Caroline was willing to sit on my lap and give me hugs and kisses. She was a happy, well-adjusted little girl with no scars.

Chapter 4

Another memorable patient was Mohammed, a Muslim man. He was in his sixties and had lived with diabetes for seventeen years. He came in with an infected foot and the big toe bone showing. He occasionally checked his blood sugar and said the numbers ranged from 400-700. He thought 400 was pretty good (normal for a person without diabetes is 70-100). He became my patient and came in every day so we could soak his foot, debride the dead tissue, spray healing oils on, cover his foot with Animal Scents ointment (a Young Living product) and wrap it up; then he'd hobble back home.

After two and a half weeks, the improvement was amazing. The infection was gone, and the hole was healing up. He was so grateful for the treatment and improvement that he presented two chickens for me to share with our team. One Saturday night we cooked the chickens for dinner and waited with great anticipation, as it smelled so good. We each tried to take a bite, but the meat was so tough you couldn't even bite it off. We all told him we enjoyed the chickens, as we did have fun watching everyone try to bite and chew the meat—lots of laughter around the table!

I was looking forward to seeing him again the next year when I went back, but got word he had died two months before I returned. That really made me sad, as we had developed a friendship over the time he'd come in. He was intelligent and could talk about many topics. When we asked if we could pray for him, he said, "You pray to your God and I'll pray to mine." I so appreciated the fact that we had been able to develop a friendship despite the cultural and religious differences. Love of fellow man can overcome a lot of prejudices.

Several years ago, because of the many infected wounds I saw coming in, I decided to try using poultices to draw out the infections. I mixed up dry oatmeal with a little water, and then added eight to ten drops of Thieves essential oil, an effective anti-infectious oil that draws out infection as well as splinters and thorns.

After mixing the poultice for a patient, I'd apply it to a gauze pad, place it on the infected area, and wrap it up. When patients returned the next day, their wounds showed much improvement because the poultice drew out the "bad stuff." This treatment has been so effective that I use the technique routinely when I'm at the clinic in Kenya.

So many children routinely come into the clinic in with coughs, runny noses, fevers, and tonsillitis that I needed to come up with an effective method of treatment. I mix up several oils to deal with respiratory issues, coughs, infections, and fevers, diluting them well, then rub the mixture all over the children's throats, chests, and backs. On babies, I rub it on their feet. Moms keep their babies bundled so well that it's a process to get them uncovered. Feet are usually the easiest way to get the oils on them.

One little boy kept his family awake every night, crying from a bad toothache. His mom brought him in to see if I could help him. I diluted clove oil in an empty bottle and she rubbed it on his bad tooth and gum area. She reported later that he slept all night and they were thankful for that oil for many nights following.

During my last week in Kenya on one of our trips, a seventy-nine-year-old lady came in with severe respiratory problems and a massive, likely a migraine, headache. She looked like she was on death's doorstep. She could hardly breathe and had no energy, the headache was about blinding her, and she had pain everywhere. After she received an antibiotic injection, I started working on her with essential oils from head to foot. I also gave her some water to drink, as she never drank water—just cow's milk or blood. I had to support her strongly to just get her out to the waiting area and then into the taxi.

Two days later, my last day in the clinic before leaving to come back home, she walked in. She looked amazing—bright-eyed, 98-percent O2 saturation, and alert—but she still had a bit of a headache and wanted more oils. After I rubbed her head and neck, I asked her if I could give her a big hug. That about did me in—I am so emotional when it comes to saying good-bye. I had to hurry to another room before breaking down, and ask God, "How can I leave these people? I love them so much!"

Every year, so many of the people there ask me to *please* come back next year because I had helped them greatly and would be sorely missed. How can I not go each year and supply what they have found to be of such help? The long hours of travel, overcoming jet lag, and dealing with my own health issues seems insignificant in comparison to their need. Lord willing, I will keep going as long as I have breath and health in my body.

Some days after clinic hours, several of us walked through the village. We ran into many kids and sang a song and clapped along with them; we saw old friends from years past and got big hugs from them; we talked and interacted with young boys who were playing with old tires up and down the road. Once an old man greeted me whom I had treated in a *manyatta* (what their home is called) a year earlier when we were visiting people around the village. He stood and waited for me to greet him—what a God moment! We couldn't understand each other, but our smiles and strong handclasps said it all. I traced my finger down the bridge of his nose where I had put lavender last year for his dry eyes, and he nodded at me. It chokes me up every time I remember that moment.

My heart is also touched when the moms bring their babies in for immunizations and we smile and talk to the babies. They watch us with their big eyes, and most will smile and react back with their baby talk. When they get their immunization shots and scream and cry, we apply an oil on that spot to take away the pain. The babies stop crying in under a minute. The moms all want us to put that peppermint on their babies when they get their shots and will gesture to get our attention if we miss one.

We often treat people coming in with trauma from fights. One man was drunk, dirty, smelly, all beat up with bruises and abrasions everywhere, and needing stitches. His jaw was swollen and possibly broken; he had received a bad blow to his chest and had a leg injury. After the doctor stitched him up, I felt as if God allowed me to "wash his feet" as I smoothed essential oils over his painful areas and cuts and cleaned him up—I felt such love for this human being who so needed God's love shown to him. Everyone else laughed at his drunken statements as I worked on him, but I was praying, asking God to truly minister to this man.

Several days later he came back in for removal of the stitches and looked like a different man. The jaw swelling was down—it was not broken—and he was back in his right mind. He wanted the oils applied again as they had helped him with the pain.

These stories—these people—are the reason I go every year. I am simply allowing God to use my hands and heart. My eyes drip with emotion as I work with the Masai, but I just want to be His vessel.

One year, after supper one night, our team was all gathered around the supper table talking when we heard a great commotion coming from the clinic. The doctor went up to see what was happening and sent word for *everyone* to come up to help. An open truck had been driving a couple dozen people home to their various villages. The vehicle was going too fast and flipped, rolling several times, throwing people all over the area. Many were badly injured, so they were all brought to the clinic, which was the only available medical care for many miles.

Every room was full of patients, and others lay on carts out in the halls. Many family members, friends, and others simply wanting to know what was going on were trying to crowd into the rooms with the patients. We had to shoo them out so we could go to work.

One clinic officer was sewing up open wounds; another was starting IVs on those needing it; triage was underway, with medical personnel taking vitals on those who were awaiting treatment. I just started in one room and put oils on every patient throughout the clinic. One big man was moaning loudly, and we couldn't tell if his neck or back was broken. I put oils everywhere I could reach skin, even on his feet. Then I moved on to the next person.

A while later, I went back into the room and found the big man had fallen asleep. The essential oils had helped his spasms relax and relieve the pain enough that he could let go and fall asleep during the chaos. We found a sheet of flexible plywood to use as a backboard, and then wrapped him up in *shugas* (big colorful blankets they all wear) to immobilize him for the trip to the hospital.

The man returned to our clinic the next week, walking with a cane, to thank us all for the great care he had received—even better than what he received at the hospital, he said. His back was not broken, just badly bruised. Several other young men came in later for more oils to be applied as they had helped greatly with their pain that night.

The evening of the accident, I saw a man lying on the floor in the corner of our big waiting room. I thought he was dead, so I worked on many other patients in the waiting room. Several of the locals I had trained in the use and administration of the oils helped me apply the oils, using cell phone lights to see where the patients were injured. We didn't have electricity in the clinic, just solar lights—which had run out of power—so we had to resort to flashlights and cell phones. I'd have never been able to cover everyone with oils if Zipporah and William hadn't helped me.

The Final Quarter

When we finally had time to go check on the person in the corner, we found he was alive. He was an eighty-five-year-old man whose son had brought him to the clinic that morning from a distant village to get oils applied on his painful joints. I had worked on the man for a long time that morning. His son was taking him back home, both of them riding in the truck when the accident happened. The poor old man was now badly banged up and really needed to have the oils applied all over again.

The young driver of the van had a compound fracture of his arm and needed surgery. Someone had started an IV on him and hung a liter of fluids to run in. The IV bag was empty, so one of his friends disconnected the tubing from the needle in his arm. I was called in to stop the blood flow because it was an open port and the blood was draining back out. What a mess all over the exam table—it took a few minutes to find a syringe to cap the port, and then I had to clean up all the blood.

One young guy had a broken ankle. He insisted he was fine and able to walk on it, but he was still in shock, so we had his friends help carry him to the car and take him to a hospital for X-rays and possible surgery.

We weren't sure if one pregnant patient from the accident still had a live fetus, as we couldn't hear fetal heart tones. The doctor felt even the baby was in shock. The next day we were able to hear them, and she retained the baby.

Another lady had a possible broken pelvis and screamed every time she moved.

Dr. Tonya took the limited supply of pain medicine we had in the pharmacy and divided it among the most badly wounded before sending them off to hospitals. I often think of the suffering all those people would have experienced while being transported to distant hospitals if our clinic hadn't been right there to give them first aid, take care of open wounds, and help minimize the trauma. God had planted the clinic and our team there for a big reason—to serve those who needed wonderful, timely medical care.

Four hours after we started on the first patient we were finished, having taken care of each patient. We had sent many out to different hospitals in far-off areas to get x-rayed or have surgery. The rest were taken home via taxi, motorcycle, or on foot.

The clinic—Ngoswani Community Health Clinic—is becoming well-known in the immediate and surrounding communities for the good care everyone receives and because it is God-based. We pray with the patients for their healing, and ask God to move mightily in their lives. The people appreciate this, as He is all they have to depend on. The oils are an absolutely vital aspect of this medical clinic, as it is truly based on being God's hand to these people, and the oils *are* God's medicines. The people recognize this and embrace the oils as natural and healing.

I could never completely describe how it feels to be in the place God has put me in Kenya, using the presents/gifts He gave me, having prepared well for just this situation. When you put your trust in the plans and purpose God created for you, there is no greater joy.

In addition to the blessing of being part of this medical clinic and using and teaching essential oils as a natural health tool, I have received the gift of new amazing relationships with people around the globe. I have also been undergirded by the amazing, unrelenting support and encouragement from my best friend and husband, Gene. In the next chapter I want you to meet and hear from some of those who've joined me on this journey.

Chapter 5

Vital Relationships

No one should do life alone. Even in our unique journeys to fulfill our purpose, we are joined by others, we impact others, and we receive encouragement and support from others. One of the greatest blessings of finding my place in serving the Masai people of Kenya is the relationships that have arisen and continue despite the distance. One of the joys of having the ability through technology to communicate with people around the world is staying in touch with my friends there. They can ask questions and encourage me, and it enables us to maintain our friendships. Technology also keeps me connected back to Gene and home when I'm away.

I love the people in our village of Ngoswani, and have adopted (unofficially) a family of nine—mom and dad with six boys and one girl. Julius is the father, a man of high standing in the Masai community and tribe. He killed three lions as a young man and has the scars to prove that one was up close and personal. He was also the project manager for New Frontiers Health Force, the mission group I work with. He oversaw all the building projects, transporting the teachers back and forth to the school the mission has built, drove to town for supplies, and anything else Dr. Tonya had for him to do. He donated land next to his family's home for

The Final Quarter

Linda and Dr. Tonya to build a school for the Masai children, so they could get a good education. He is thrilled to see the school now growing from forty-five to seventy-nine kids. They are building another big classroom, dining room, and kitchen area.

Zipporah is his wife and a wonderful, godly woman with a quiet, loving spirit. She is a leader in the community as well, teaching Bible studies with the women. When needed, she helps with the team members' laundry, cleans the clinic daily, and has raised six boys and one girl. After all those boys—Joseph, Jeremiah, Michael, James, Leymian, and Samuel—they finally had a girl, Abigail. She is surrounded by boys, so she is a tomboy and able to hold her own.

Over the last ten years, I have watched the kids grow up and leave for boarding school. The last two at home, Samuel and Abigail, will leave in a couple of years. I am happy these young people are getting a good education, but sad as I never seem to be there when their schools are out and they are home. I miss our interaction and talks. I never got to know Joseph, as he had already gone off to school when I started my trips to Ngoswani. Each boy was unique, and as the older ones left for school, I had more time with the ones left. I grew to love each one of them.

In the early years, we were able to go exploring around the area if a couple of the Masai accompanied us. The kids loved showing us their surroundings—the water holes, skulls and dried bones lying around from the droughts—and introducing us to their friends in the different manyattas. Of course, the kids all wanted their pictures taken and then had to see the digital photos in our cameras. A few years later our explorations were curtailed as the area began to get more dangerous. Missionaries were abducted, more refugees moved to the village, and animals attacked people on the roads. We are cautious now; we travel in pairs and must let our whereabouts be known at all times.

Chapter 5

One of the fun parts of being on the NFHF team is all the friends you make. The first year I went, in 2008, I met Linda Brown, a videographer and photographer who worked at a TV station. She planned to take pictures and videos of the work Dr. Tonya was doing. We had to share a king-sized bed and another nurse shared our room on a twin bed. Linda and I both struggled going to sleep, so she finally admitted she'd gotten a sleeping pill from a nurse and asked if I wanted half. She divided it with me, and we talked and laughed as quietly as possible to keep from waking up all the other occupants. It became our nightly routine to ask each other if we'd been able to "borrow" a sleeping pill and then divide it.

It is crazy, but the only time I ever need a pill to go to sleep is in Africa! You always hear animal noises outside, the sounds of the Masai people walking behind the dorm building to cross the river below us, and the barking of the three compound dogs. If one of them hears something, it starts barking or howling and the other two join in and "sing" for several minutes. Abruptly they will stop, and you think you can go to sleep—then they do it again. It can be noisy at night.

We lie in bed and listen to the hyenas make their waa-hoop sound through the night. Sometimes they are quite close. One night I had gone to the bathroom around 2:00 a.m. when I heard a hyena so loud it sounded as if it was right outside the door. I was so scared I couldn't even open the door and just stood there listening. A few minutes later, Dr. Tonya came up to the bathroom and I felt safe again. I *love* the adventure but at times it can be unnerving.

Linda quit her television job of twenty-five years in Florida and became an intern with Dr. Tonya in 2009 to become a missionary, and she now works alongside Dr. Tonya. She founded Linda's Kids Academy, which now has over ninety students. They plan to add a grade each year, so the kids can stay there for all their schooling until they graduate. This alone has made a great impact on the community. Their kids are now able to receive excellent education. All of the village's young students at the academy tested very high in the yearly government testing that local schools must administer.

Cheryl is another friend who was with me in Kenya four different years, so we bonded and had great times together. One year we roomed together in the back room and would talk and laugh until time to go to sleep. One morning she woke up early and asked me, "What time is it?"

Well, I had to find my watch under my pillow, then find my glasses somewhere on my bed, then find a light so I could read what it said, and then I told her.

"That only took you fifteen minutes," she said, followed by a snide inference that I was getting old and couldn't see anymore.

She went on out to the bathroom—and soon I heard her rattling the door next to us. She came in a few minutes later and said, "I'll never think you are old again."

She had been trying to enter an empty room and couldn't understand why the door was locked. She thought we were playing a trick on her. We started laughing, and the more we thought about it, the funnier it got. We were practically howling, and I had to keep stuffing the pillow over my face to stifle the noise. We'd try to settle down and then just look at each other and start laughing again. The nurse in the next room to ours went outside thinking someone was hurt and crying out there—until she found us. I know—you had to be there to see how it could be so funny, but even now I laugh whenever I think about it.

One year I was sitting on the front stoop of our team's building, talking with another team member and Michael, one of my "grandsons." We heard two dogs barking and it sounded *strange*. We looked up to see a hooded head sticking up out of the grass maybe thirty to forty feet away. I asked Michael, "Is that a cobra?"

"Yes," he answered, and threw rocks to drive the dogs away. "Go into your room and close the door," he said, to get me away from potential trouble.

But I didn't want to miss the action, so I said, "No way!"

Michael went to get salt from the kitchen, explaining how they pour it around the hole where the snakes live to eventually kill them by desiccation (drying out). We saw the cobra's head once again, but then couldn't find it. Some of the adult men came to help look. It happened right by the path where we all walked to the different compound buildings, so it was a bit unnerving to think a cobra was so close by. We were unable to locate it at that time. So when I went out to brush my teeth at night with my toothbrush and a bottle of water, I had my headlight flashing all around the tree and grass to make sure the snake didn't sneak up on me. Later, Julius, our project manager found a cobra under some boards in his shed and killed it with a shovel. We prayed that was the one we'd seen earlier.

The Cobras of Life

As I contemplated that scenario, it reminded me how we act or react to situations in our own lives. We might have some warning signs of something wrong (dogs barking), and can either pay attention or choose to ignore them. Suddenly a serious event or threat happens (cobra rearing its head), like a heart attack, car wreck, serious health issue like cancer, or serious relationship problem, and we are forced to either address it or run away.

How do *you* handle a cobra in your life? Do you face it with courage or try to suppress it as if it is not really happening? You do realize it can bite you in the butt in the future if you ignore it, don't you? Also, what kind of salt—or treatment—do you use to deal with the issue? I want to talk to you more about that in a later chapter.

The Final Quarter

When a serious situation occurs, it makes you much more alert and watchful of something else developing, until enough time has gone by that you feel more comfortable and relax your vigil. That event will always be a part of you and lay dormant in your memory, but raise its head if the threat ever arises again. Anxiety can eat away at you as you anticipate the worst, or you can learn to put your worries and fears in the hands of the One who can watch over you and take care of it.

One of my favorite verses that speaks to this is:

God is our refuge and strength, an ever-present help in trouble.
—Psalm 46:1

One of my Masai friends, Ann, has been a translator for us for a number of years and is also an accomplished seamstress, sewing dresses *without any patterns*. She set up her own shop to support her family and herself. She tells another story of unexpected trouble. She was in bed one night and felt something move under her sheet. She knelt on the other side of the bed and prayed for God to protect her. The next morning as she was making her bed and fluffed the sheet up, she saw a deadly black Mamba snake under the sheet. She screamed and ran out to find some men to come in to kill it.

I admire people who live with danger in all aspects of their lives. There are wild animals all around and few fences in the Masai village. To protect themselves, the people surround a group of homes with thorny bushes to help keep out wild animals, and they bring their herds of cattle, sheep, and goats into the enclosure to protect them at night.

A leopard killed a man not far from our compound where the road crosses the river. Elephants have been known to kill people as they cross their path. Water buffalo are exceedingly dangerous and have injured many people when they bring their animals to drink in the river. The buffalo will attack without provocation and cause extensive bodily damage. We had many patients with serious injuries from water buffalo on my most recent trip, as a drought caused the animals to guard their river territory aggressively. Anyone just trying to cross the river can be attacked.

At night, lions roam around, as do zebra, hyenas, leopards, giraffe, elephants, and other wild animals. In the past, young Masai men would have to prove their bravery by killing a lion. Whoever did so wore the mane to show his standing as a brave warrior. Now killing lions is outlawed—unless the lions are aggressively killing the animals in a herd—as they are declining in numbers.

The Masai's wealth is in their flocks and herds, which they are unwilling to sell unless necessary. As a result, many people live on pennies a day. We have no idea how blessed we are in America, even those who live at poverty level, with all of our resources, jobs, and available assistance.

Training the Locals

In 2016 I travelled to another village four hours away from ours to stay with my good friends Kari and Randy Saul, who have a ministry in Kebabe Village, close to Kisii Town. While staying a week with them, I was able to apply the oils on many people. I was with them over Easter Sunday, so Pastor Randy told the people about the oils and that I was willing to help them with their needs. After the church service, I sat on one of the wooden benches in the church, with sawdust floors and tarp coverings over the sides to let in air and light, and the people came to talk to me. I was able to apply oils on them to help support their bodies with their health issues. They loved the oils and the soothing effects and healing they provided.

In 2017 I went back to the village for the second time, and people came to the house asking for oils for their health issues. I was able to train a local lady in how to use the oils on everyone. She came early and stayed late to follow us around the village ministering to the people. We had many with infected cuts on legs and fingers, sore backs and joints, etc. I was able to leave a year's supply of the essential oils for their use. From time to time, I hear from her about how the people keep her busy asking for the oils. She sometimes texts me with questions about how to deal with certain situations. I was so thankful to be able to train someone and leave a supply of oils so the people there can have this help all year long.

One experience that impacted my heart was in February 2017 when two translators came to see me the night before I left, asking if I would go and train someone in each of their villages so the people could have access to the essential oils. They have very poor and sparse health care coverage in much of Kenya, especially out in the bush and smaller villages. Their request put such a desire in my heart to educate a key person in several villages, supplying them with oils to cover needs for a year, and then to go back each year to further educate and restock oils. As the number of my chronological years keeps adding up, my need is to find and teach someone to take over this ministry—to get the oils and then take them to these various villages. We need to keep educating others in the use and application of essential oils, so people's health can be impacted naturally.

A Passion for Kenya

My taxi driver, Nahason, said he is praying that God will turn my years back and I will keep getting younger, so I can keep coming to Kenya. For a number of years, he has driven me from village to village, and then to Nairobi to catch my plane, and as we travel for hours we talk about many things—his home and family situation, my home and family, political situations in both of our countries, and of course how God is working in our lives. A couple of times, he told me to lie back and sleep, as he would take good care of me and get me safely to where I was going. Such care and love I receive from these people.

As I get older, I find the long travel times take longer to rebound from. It currently takes almost two full days (with three to four flights and layovers) to get from Tampa to Nairobi. The airlines may eventually offer flights more directly from Tampa to Nairobi and cut down on some of the different segments of the trip—I'm hoping!

This quarter of my life is proving to be so full and eventful, as though I have come out of a box with its protective shell around me. I have ventured halfway around the world to follow the call God has put on my life. I can only stand in amazement at what He has allowed me to see and experience. Many times, when I get on a plane, it seems the person I sit next to is a divine appointment. They allow me to see into their life, circumstances, and needs. I then share what God has done and is still doing in my life, and how He has given me a tool to minister to people physically.

One year I was getting ready to go on a trip to Kenya, and the impulse to write a letter to the planes' captains came on me strongly. Though it was late, and I had just a few hours to sleep, I *had* to get up and write it. I didn't know if the message was for one specific person who was struggling with the job becoming ho-hum, but I made copies to give to each captain. It felt as if God wanted me to share a message with one specific person to minister to them. I didn't know who or why, but that didn't matter. I just did it. Here is what I wrote:

Dear Captain,

This is simply a letter of gratitude! I just want to thank you for your careful and competent handling of your job in getting so many people to different places around the world! We file onto your plane, and then file off after landing, and never really get a chance to say a proper "Thank you" for a job well done. You, and your whole crew, do a top-notch job of taking care of us.

Some days it may seem like just another day at work, and even a bit humdrum or boring; or you may be feeling a bit under the weather, or depressed over relationships with others; *or* you may just love your job and can't wait to get to it each time you fly!

Whatever—I want you to know that what you do impacts thousands upon thousands of people each time you fly a big trip with all of us. Each person on your flight is a story in and unto himself, and you will never know the richness of the human factor simply because your job is to stay in your cockpit and fly the plane. Each one of us touches so many lives; you multiply that by the number of people on the plane—and you get the picture.

I was lying in bed Saturday night, trying to go to sleep to get ready for two days of travel, and God impressed upon my heart to write and say "Thank you," instead of me just thanking God for the different abilities He has given to people to help others. I have never done this before, but I am getting bolder in my old age!

I am traveling with a group of ten people going to Kenya on a month-long medical mission, working with the Masai out in the bush. This is my fifth year of doing this, and I have grown to love these people deeply, and cannot wait to see them all again. I am a nurse anesthetist, but because we don't have electricity or running water in the village where we go, we just do basic health care. I work with a doctor from Clearwater, Florida, who has done medical missions for nineteen years in over twenty-seven countries. We built a medical clinic in the village we go to, along with a church, and staff housing. We are now going to build another church and a one-room clinic waaaaay out in the bush to try to meet basic medical needs of over seven thousand people who have no health care at all. I also use essential oils on many of the people, and they now call me "Oils Mama."

So, when I say we each impact many people, I want you to know that there are many Masai in Kenya who are being touched because you got us to our destination safely. We may seem like nameless faces that pass by you quickly, but your work is *very* important to each one of us.

I so appreciate your knowledge and abilities in your specialized field, as you would if you needed my services in my specialized field.

Please let your crew know that we are truly thankful for their help and care of each one of us.

A grateful passenger,

Sue Heath

As I reflect on this third quarter of life, especially as I have pursued my place of service in Kenya, I have realized that none of this could have happened without my husband's blessing and willingness to let me go for five weeks at a time to answer this call on my heart. He keeps our home fires burning and conducts his own business, works on many projects around the house, and takes notes when I call once a week to tell of my adventures. He then sends out emails to those who are waiting for the latest news, telling them what's happened, and adds his own inimitable storytelling style and his own news. Here are a few examples:

Sue's Kenya, week 1:

Momma Oils has landed. She called yesterday. She was supposed to call at 8 a.m., but forgot and remembered at 1 p.m. It was good to get reacquainted with her and jog her memory as to who I am after only four days of separation. Her arrival at the Nairobi airport was a page out of the stooges as she and Dr. Tonya (they are now traveling as Curly and Moe) got separated. Sue thought Tonya had gotten off the plane first as they were not seated together. Tonya was close to the plane door and Sue was closer to the back. After waiting and not seeing Tonya, Sue proceeded to go through the line for visa inspection. So when Tonya got off she thought Sue was following (big mistake as Sue is not a follower, as we all know). Tonya waited until the crew debarked and figured Sue was on the move. Sue, meanwhile, had gotten her baggage, and after looking all over and not finding Tonya, had proceeded through customs. Then still not finding Tonya, she assumed she was outside getting transportation, so out the door she went, only to find that there was no Tonya—and of course there is now no turning back. To re-enter you have to go through customs and repeat the whole check-in process. She finally went back into the airport and ultimately reunited with Moe, who was in a state of panic, thinking all sorts of disasters had happened to Curly. Well, Moe and Curly got outside and decided to simply breathe and take their valium until their color subsided from brilliant red to more normal pink. Without Sue's cell phone activated for Kenya, there was no way for them to communicate.

Chapter 5

They finally got to the place where they stay before going out to their village. They also had a pizza meal with the Moores (our Keystone-sponsored Nairobi missionaries) who Tonya had not met before. Then yesterday they went to the market to buy school uniforms for the students at the clinic compound. They have forty-five students. They were joined yesterday by Andrea RN from Illinois. The three of them will be the entire staff at the clinic this week, as the rest of the staff was given the week off for R&R. Their project manager, Julius, will be their driver to the clinic.

Since Sue left, the house is suddenly much larger and less congested. I haven't bumped into anyone in the hallway, kitchen, or bathroom. The phone has gone silent. And all the things I put down stay where I put them. I don't think I'm losing my mind anymore. But things will change when Curly gets back.

Blessings, Gene

Sue's Kenya, week 2:

I got a call an hour early today. I think Sue finally appreciates my value and misses me. She said the clinic was well staffed last week as the regular staff had stayed on instead on taking the week off since she, Andrea, and Dr. Tonya had gotten there late last Monday. So the staff will take this week off, and the new team will take over. They did do a school clothing fitting. That must have been an exciting time for the students. Sue also taught some sessions on essential oil use to the staff.

The news in the village was that a lion had killed some goats and sheep. So, the herdsmen were burning the surrounding brushy areas to try to make it more difficult for the lions to sneak up on the herds. The resulting smoke also made it more difficult to breathe at the clinic and in their rooms at night. The other news was that the project manager (Julius) owns a pregnant cow, which is near the end of her term. She has become weak and would rather lie down than stand (I know how she feels). Unfortunately, when she lies down, she can't get up by herself. It takes eleven men to help her get up, which is an effort, as those of you know if you've ever lifted a cow. So, they have her staying at the compound by Julius's house to try to fortify her diet and keep an eye on her when she delivers.

They received a couple of rain showers to settle the dust. Their seasons are opposite of ours, so the rainy season should begin soon. They have a new kitchen, which is a great addition. They are working on a dining area now.

Here at home I can't believe how many care packages have come. None. It's a good thing I like ice cream bars and fruit for rations as I can keep them in stock. I steam cleaned the rugs, did roof work, and installed a water filter this week. So even in a weakened state I carry on.

Blessings, Gene

Sue's Kenya, week 3:

Sue called from outside the clinic under the night sky with a spectacular view of the stars, including the Milky Way. She was also under a large wasp nest, which she was hoping would remain calm. They had a busy week with two major medical cases. One was with a man who had been crossing a stream and was gored in the groin by a water buffalo. He also had some rib, hip, and leg damage. They attended his wounds and sewed him up for transport to a hospital a couple of hours away. Another case involved a pregnant woman who was in labor for nine hours. She finally delivered the baby, but it was having breathing difficulties. So it was transported to the hospital also.

Her other excitement was a safari trip where they had to travel over a poorly maintained narrow bridge. They proceeded to cross and a rear wheel fell through a hole in the bridge. The vehicle had to then be winched out to the other side. The driver had to tighten the noisy wheels, but there still was noise coming from the engine. While they were out driving in the Mara, the engine stopped. He found the fan belt had broken and had to replace it with a spare. (This is what we all would do since we normally carry spare belts.) I asked Sue if she got out of the vehicle when its wheel went through the bridge. She responded with, "No, you don't get out of the vehicle when you're on safari"—so I guess it's better to go down with the ship than be a meal on foot. Just as they got back to the compound, the vehicle lost a fitting on the drive shaft and wouldn't move farther. She looked under the jeep and the drive shaft was lying on the ground! That was the excitement from the safari. We didn't even talk about the animal life they saw, as she was just happy to get back safely. Can you believe she was more excited about the trip itself than the animal sightings?!

They went to church today and the pastor announced that Dr. Tonya was there and would preach the sermon. This was a surprise to Tonya, but she rallied to the occasion. The attendance at church was down as the people with herds must move them away to areas with grazing due to the severe drought in the area. Sue asked that you pray for rain to ease the drought. If they don't get some relief soon the herds will start to die off. The pregnant cow from the last report gave birth to a cute brown calf. The cow is regaining her strength, and the number of men required to get the cow up has decreased from eleven to four. They use ropes under the cow and a tree limb for leverage.

Friday night they were trying to get to sleep but a nearby church was playing music so loud they couldn't sleep. I hope our pastor doesn't turn up the church volume to keep me awake. That is so annoying! They have taken walks around the compound with the company of the three compound sentinel dogs. It turns out the dogs are attack dogs and have killed a neighbor's goat. The dogs also try to eliminate the two compound cats, who must run or climb for their lives. The most aggressive dog has taken a shine to Sue—probably thinks she is an alpha female!

I received a sympathy card (Mawhinneys) exhorting me to remain strong, a person at church saying they forgot my care package (how is that possible?), and a great lunch with the Dunkerlys. So I'm good for this week.

Blessings, Gene

Sue's Kenya, week 4:

She misses me after-all. She called a little early this morning to tell me so. She has six more days at the clinic before heading to Kari and Randy Saul's place four hours away. They are doing mission work in the uplands of Kenya. They have developed a chicken business to employ the local people there. The goal is to bring them into a productive program (after going through U-Turn to turn them away from drugs and alcohol toward Christ). Sue was there last year to begin introducing people to the essential oils health treatment.

The village and consequently the clinic are in a slow period due to the people being away with their herds seeking grazing areas. Still no significant rain, and the local grass had been drought ravaged. They had three injured from water buffalo last week. The buffalo are protecting their limited water holes and attack anyone who ventures near. They had one twelve-year-old come in with a broken hip or leg and bleeder, which they tied off. Then he was transported to the hospital and hour and a half away. They also had several births. One stillborn to a woman who was on her ninth birth. Another to a woman on her first whose birth canal was too small for delivery so she had to be transported to hospital for a C-section. She was resistant to the idea of surgery until Dr. Tonya told her the baby would die, and then she would die also. She and the baby did well. The hospital equipment is not the most reliable, and they had to provide backup support. The regular staff at the hospital has been on strike for nearly two months. I'm not a fan of going to the hospital even when they are fully staffed and everything works—guess I'll stay here!

By the way, Sue did see some wildlife on her safari a week ago—elephants, hippos (who were under a layer of crud on the water trying to stay cool), lion with three cubs, giraffes, and hyenas. She got close enough to the hyenas to be scared by their nasty-looking teeth.

During the slow times at the clinic Sue has been admonished to just relax. That is not a word in Sue's vocabulary, and she does not understand its meaning. She is much more likely to create some sort of diversionary activity—I know the look that she gets in her eye when she thinks I have been inactive too long.

My church friends are coming to my aid. Guilt can be a beautiful thing to observe in the church family when it finally results in action. So the Johnsons came through with a care package of goodies. I can take them off my forgiveness list now. My board meeting last week with sixteen governments went well as they decided it was better to work together than go it alone. They approved three contracts to develop and conserve future water supplies for the next twenty-plus years. That is a miracle for sure. I told my technical/legal team that it is rare in one's career to actually be a participant in such an event—to be thankful.

Blessings, Gene

Sue's Kenya, week 5:

My last "Sue's epistle"—at least for this year. She will return next Sunday night after 11 p.m. I'm not worried about forgetting her arrival, but hope I stay awake for it. I'll have to look at some pictures of her to make sure I've not forgotten what she looks like. She called today from Kebabe Village, which is about four hours away from her medical clinic. This is the Sauls' mission where she is staying this week. They finally have received a few days of rain, so the extreme drought is easing, and things are greening up rapidly. The sky was darkening, and thunder was in the distance as we talked.

Before she left the clinic, the big events of the week included when a bat entered the room where Sue and Andrea were watching a movie and was quickly greeted with the hysterical inhabitants—Sue and Andrea. Dr. Tonya ran to see what the ruckus was about from Andrea screaming, and couldn't believe a single little bat had Sue lying back on a chair laughing hysterically as the bat kept dive-bombing her. Dr. Tonya just stood there and then waved the bat out the door! (I used to keep a tennis racket handy when we lived in Pennsylvania for such occasions.) Besides, Tonya had better things to do as she and a staffer had needed to fix a dripping faucet. So in an effort to fix it, the entire faucet came off, and with it they emptied their storage of hot water into buckets and pans. They all quickly took hot spitz baths! Their van had a tire blow out, and Tonya's vehicle has its maintenance light on continuously. The wear and tear on the vehicles is harsh. However, on a positive note, they did manage to deliver a healthy 9lb baby, which Sue thought was a pretty hefty sized baby compared to the norm for the clinic.

So back to the Sauls' mission. I had mentioned in an earlier report that they have developed a chicken business for employing the people there. They are in the process of building several new coops to increase the number of chickens to 5,000. With the rain, not only is the grass greening but the chicken fertilizer is even more aromatic than before. Sue was having sinus trouble before because of the dust and smoke, and now she is enjoying (?) the aroma of wet fertilizer that permeates the compound. She offered to bring me a bottle of fertilizer home for my enjoyment, but I informed her that being raised on a farm with chicken coops, the aroma does not really make me feel nostalgic. That chapter of my life can remain closed.

Friday, she will be heading for the Moores in Nairobi to stay one night and clean up before starting her trip back.

She has a three-hour layover in Amsterdam and a six-hour layover in Detroit. On the home front I have been busy consulting and doing some projects around the house. I had dinners with the Dudgeons and Mawhinneys. I am thankful for caring friends. Now I've got to go watch the Super Bowl.

Blessings, Gene

People write back to Gene and tell him he provided a note of sunshine and laughter to their day with his epistles; they look forward to his note every Saturday and say he should write a book about life with me! He *does* have a dry sense of humor.

I am so thankful for my family's love, care, and support. They don't get stressed about me leaving for a period of time every year, and now just ask me when I am going this year.

A Passion for Life

While my Kenya trips and taking the oils to the Masai people is the most significant part of this second half of my third quarter, I've also been busy at home. Another big accomplishment this quarter is I learned about social media and how to use it with my business of educating people about the essential oils; promoting the use of ZYTO scans to find areas of stress in the body and EVOX scans to help give voice to your emotions and perception reframing; and using Raindrop Technique for health support. I and another friend, Lisa, sell Raindrop Belts and Equine Kits on Etsy to help make the Raindrop process easier, simpler, and faster when doing it on either people or horses. Horses love the oils being applied on them. Oils on animals is a whole other field.

Coming from a medical background and being business illiterate, I needed help to process all I was learning and determine how to put it all into action. A couple of my mentors have helped me greatly—Celestine Herbert with her Godsperity Business Building Program, and Steve Hopper with his Like a Boss series. He is the one who encouraged me to put my life experiences down in book form, and has also helped me learn how to put together speaking presentations. They have both helped give direction to my desire to build a business to help support the different missions and missionaries that I love, and to put feet to my dreams.

These are mentors who helped me see the mental blocks I have been dealing with; to look at the beliefs I have about money and whether I deserve to make some; to decide who I am targeting to work with; to learn different ways to use social media; and what to spend my time and focus, as well as money, on.

If you struggle with growing your business, I encourage you to spend the money for help through mentors, coaches, and workshops. It really is *investing* the money to help you learn and grow in the right way and direction.

As I look back on the first three quarters of my life, I am amazed at the way my experiences have not only defined who I am but also who I will be as I keep moving forward. From raising children, to all my experiences in the medical field, to surviving menopause, and realizing my purpose and gifts for mission work—all of these things have come together to make me who I am. These experiences pull me to go back every year to minister to more people. This allows me to rekindle the relationships that have been established simply because they see I care enough to come back year after year. I have been blessed, exceedingly abundantly beyond what I could ever think or dream, through each one's life. Any impact I might have is greatly exceeded by the impact they've had on me. I am truly a blessed woman.

I wonder, have you ever stopped . . . just to think back and see the defining moments in your own life, and are then able to see how they have guided you in the decisions you have made and where you are today? Have you appreciated the richness of those experiences—both good and bad—to recognize that you might not have developed into the person you are today if those times hadn't been a part of your life? Maybe you think of the bad times as negative, but if you are honest, can you see how they have been a part of the character development that you have today, and that some good has come about because of those times? Honestly, I wouldn't have come to my own understanding if someone hadn't challenged me to write a book about my life and forced me to take a hard look at how God was directing it all along the way. So, I'm challenging you—find your *defining moments* and evaluate your life. What do you want to do with the rest of it?

I can only look back in amazement at how full my life has become as I've grown older. I don't know if I'm aging gracefully or fighting it tooth and nail! I just want to accomplish all I can in the time I have allotted. I don't think too much about it—I just keep my head down and keep moving forward.

How about you? Do you have this drive in you to do more, or are you looking forward to just being able to sit back and relax? I don't think either way is wrong; you just have to know what you desire, and my desire is to keep moving forward. So what is ahead for you in your final quarter of life? Let's take a look.

The Fourth Quarter
Ages 76–100

This fourth and final quarter can be *the pinnacle* of our lives, as the work of our hands/bodies/minds all come to fruition and we can enjoy the fruit of our labors. We can either spend it in the doctor/tests/treatments/drugs/surgeries/physical therapy cycle, or spend it doing what we have desired to do—traveling, relaxing, meeting new friends, enjoying the old ones, taking family on vacations, and enjoying our present levels of health and energy. We can pour our lives into others, teaching them what we have learned and experienced in our lifetime. We can serve those less privileged and experience a joy from being selfless. We can look at the legacy we are leaving and improve it even more. It's a time of fulfillment in many areas.

Chapter 6

Fourth Quarter—The Finishing 2018–43

Old age is like a plane flying through a storm. Once you are aboard there is nothing you can do.
—Golda Meir

The fourth quarter is here! Some may have already settled into a retirement life routine and don't have any sense of productivity. Maybe they feel they've already paid their dues. Some may be thinking the end is near. In any case, the last quarter of life can be some of the best times of life.

We are entering an unknown time. It can be full of promise, possibilities, and even mystery. We have gone through our "programmed time" of growing up, getting an education, starting a job, finding a spouse, getting married, having kids, getting them educated, and seeing them off into their own futures. Now, *now* is our time to go, do, see, and be what we'd like to be and do. The restraints are off!

We have time freedom, money freedom, and the knowledge and ability to do so many things. I recognize that many don't have this freedom because of health issues, family responsibilities, or other different situations, but even so, our lives generally have more freedom.

Why do so many people lack that sense of fourth-quarter freedom? It seems the soil of our life has been packed down with the weight of all the years, responsibilities, obligations, and expectations. Some may find it hard to break through that thick crust, that we ourselves have allowed to develop, in order to achieve real freedom. It will take determination, thinking, planning, and purpose to break free of the heavy layers over our lives.

We can stimulate our brains again in so many ways, to experience new vistas, to inject a sense of joy with which to greet each new day. What are we waiting for? Are you willing to just sit and watch news/sports/sitcoms/movies every day and night, and then go to bed, only to get up and do it all over again the next day? Where is the joy, excitement, and sense of expectation in that?

I want to experience so many more places in the United States, Canada, Alaska, and all around the world. I want to meet people and experience their cultures; watch more animals in their natural habitats; go white-water rafting; take a river cruise; travel the Mississippi River on a steamboat; drive again through the south part of Utah, as that terrain is amazing. The possibilities are endless. Why do we entrap ourselves in our cubes of safety, known as our homes? I encourage you to step out and let yourself experience the feeling of fear or unease in going forth into the unknown. We need to get our blood flowing again, and not just settle down waiting to die.

Living life on your own terms is key to dying without too many regrets. If you are afraid to step out and do it on your own, find a group or club that travels or explores regularly and go with them. Take your spouse and head out on weekend exploratory drives to find out-of-the-way places that are quaint and full of history. Vacation together with another couple and enjoy the time, fellowship, and fun.

Chapter 6

Two factors that contribute to longevity are maintaining a strong social network of family and friends, and keeping your sense of humor. So exercise those factors in your life. Don't die before it is time! God still has a purpose and plan for you to accomplish.

For I know the plans I have for you, says the Lord. They are plans for good and not for evil, to give you a future and a hope.
—Jeremiah 29:11 TLB

There really is no going back to when we were younger, when we had more energy and stamina, and less wrinkles and body parts sagging south. So we must simply face forward and embrace the freedom that comes with not having to go to a nine-to-five job; no kids around to raise (although some grandparents *are* raising their kids' kids), a bit more money freedom, and the advantage of all the knowledge stored in our brains, as well as experience in life.

As I'm about to slip under the wire to hit the last quarter of my life, I want to continue doing what I'm doing now. I want to consult with people, using my "tools" to help with health issues; speak to groups about aging and what you can do to keep on living and make the rest of your life the best of your life and have optimal health; love on and live life with my family; and travel to places where there is a need for natural healing tools and where I can minister God's love to people through my hands.

Did you know the word *retire* is not in the Bible? Where did that come from—the government? What happens when people look forward so much to retiring? They feel they have earned the right to just sit back and do nothing, and soon find themselves struggling with boredom. If you just sit around, you may lose your zest for life and have no real purpose for getting out of bed. Some die early from heart attacks and never get to enjoy the fruits of all their years of labor (and I wonder if some of these could've had more years if they'd stayed active and lived with purpose). Others try to find substitutes for activity in shopping, cruises, golf, tennis, etc.—which is fine to a degree, but there are so many ways to continue to contribute to a world in need of our knowledge and experience, or give our time to minister help to those who have no one else to lend a helping hand. There is so much we can still do!

Stage Seven to a Meaningful Final Quarter: *Passion*

What exactly is passion? People throw this term around a lot these days. And the way some people talk about their passion(s), you might think they have about a dozen or more. Passion, for me, is where my path, purpose, preparation, presents, place, and perseverance intersect. We've looked at the steps to finding our ultimate fulfillment in life, and I believe passion is the key step. Once you know what you're gifted to do, how to prepare yourself to use it, the dreams you had in your past, and the place God is calling you to use those gifts, you've found your passion.

Passion is ultimately about serving others. It's feeling excitement about how and who and where you serve, pressing on with fervor and persistence despite obstacles, and having a sense of joy as you serve.

What is your passion? If you know, what are you doing to follow it, to live it out in this fourth quarter of your life? If you're not sure, take a look at the previous stages and see if you can find the intersection of them all to discover your true passion. Then ask God to show you where to go to use it in serving others.

Chapter 6

I have gained much medical knowledge over fifty-four years of nursing with thirty-nine years as a certified registered nurse anesthetist. I also gained a lot of experience in ministering to people. God has equipped me with His natural medicines, which are safe, effective, and healthy for people. This is the "tool" He has given me to impact the world—His oils. It has become my passion as I look toward this last quarter of life.

He gives us all gifts, so what is your "oil"? What tool have you been given to impact those in your sphere of influence? Are you using it? Are you consciously trying to make a difference in others' lives? If you're not, allow yourself some time for introspection to look more closely at your life, to see what your defining moments have been and how they weave your story together. See if you can find that natural ability or special gift that makes you stand out from the rest of the crowd. That is what God has given you. Use it.

My Next Adventure

As I complete this book, I am preparing to take my first missions trip to Uganda. I will join Nancy Degan, a nurse I met at a social networking meeting. She works with women in Uganda making jewelry. Nancy brings it home to sell so she can then use the money to help support the women who made it. We are both going to speak at a nurses' conference and minister to nurses who help young women make wise reproductive health and life choices. Nancy will speak on developing leadership skills in their lives. My goal is to teach the nurses about using essential oils to help their patients in the hospitals, and in health clinics out in the bush. We are being hosted by one of the nurse leaders in Kampala, Juliet Kigoona. I will visit two or three different hospitals to evaluate the need and see how they can use the oils there, teaching one person, who can then teach others. In addition, I will travel to two nursing schools to talk to the nurses-in-training about natural ways to deal with health issues.

Another group that Juliet and her friends are ministering to is young women who need to learn a skill to support themselves and a possible child or children. These women are learning to make special Ugandan terra cotta pendants, earrings, and bracelets, which Nancy has designed to help subsidize income for these young girls. Nancy sells the jewelry in the States, then takes the money back to provide a small income for these girls. We will work alongside Juliet to also teach the women how to start mini-entrepreneur endeavors, such as raising chickens or rabbits, growing mushrooms, sewing, etc.

Don't Waste the Final Quarter

I don't want to waste my time here on earth in selfish pursuit of pleasure while so many are in need. You just have to look around to find your own mission field right where you live. Time is short—I want to use it wisely and go until I can't go anymore. Then I will sit back and do another work—praying for those who can still go and for those still out there on the field serving.

This is how I want to finish this game of life—that my last quarter would be the culmination of all that God has put within me, and given me to work with. I want to be an example for my family, and leave a legacy that will imprint on their hearts. I want them to see that it doesn't matter how old you are—as long as you have breath you can do *something* to serve Him. I want to hear, "Well done, thou good and faithful servant" when I stand before Him at the Judgment Seat.

Have you thought about your own plans when you reach the final quarter of your life? Have you started looking for areas that interest you, and where you can fill a big need? Are there places you want to travel to—for pleasure and exploration or to serve in some measure with the people there? Do you want to teach at a community college, write a book, or make videos to share your expertise in some field? Opportunities are everywhere.

As you consider your final quarter, what I've talked about may be difficult for you. Perhaps you face challenges that hold you back. Let's look next at the issues and challenges that come along with our final quarter. If we can find ways to face and overcome these challenges, we can continue to follow our passions further and farther than we may think possible.

Chapter 7

Challenges Faced in Aging

One of the problems we face entering the fourth quarter of life is the increase in *mental, emotional, and physical challenges* as we age. We can let these challenges overcome us so that we stop being productive and active, or we can meet the challenges head-on and work through them whenever possible in order to keep contributing to our community and our world as long as possible.

Life definitely changes as we age. Many have to start dealing with bodily aches and pains—which can become the focus of their lives as each week becomes a round of different doctors for different ailments, to get different prescriptions to take at different times.

No wonder our friends don't have time to get together with us to go out to eat—their lives have been overtaken by the "doctor's office/drugs/surgeries/physical therapy/treatments" wheel.

You know you're getting old when all the names in your black book have M.D. after them.
—Harrison Ford

The Challenges of Aging

I have to laugh at the conversations of some older people—discussing their latest surgery, whether they had a bowel movement that day or last week, how hard it is to get up out of chairs anymore, what they've had to eat, etc. The focus at the end of our lives seems to be all on the physical. This seems backward to me—we are getting closer to meeting our maker and we should be more attuned to Him and looking forward to the day we meet Him face-to-face. That seems to have fallen off our radar in the face of more present, immediate concerns.

So that I could learn to focus more on God than myself in this final quarter, I made a list of some of the challenges we may face in this time of our lives.

Forgetfulness

- Forgetting what I walked into a room for, or where I laid my keys, checkbook, glasses, purse, important papers, etc.—(you can add your own items to the list)—and then getting sidetracked with something else to do.

   Someone sent me a story from the Internet that hit me right between the eyes as it so described me. A lady decided at breakfast that she would clean off her desk, so she went to her office and started moving her papers into piles. She came across an article she wanted to put on the counter for her husband, so took it to the kitchen. While there she decided to do the dishes. She put things away and looked in the refrigerator and saw things she needed from the store. She decided to run to the store to stock up so she put on her jacket, but then couldn't find her keys. She looked through her purse, but couldn't find them, so decided to clean out her purse.

Chapter 7

Some things dropped and spilled on the floor, so she decided to sweep the rug. While getting the sweeper out, she hit her jacket pocket and heard her car keys. So instead of sweeping, she decided to run to the store. As she walked outside to her car, she saw weeds growing in the flowerbeds and stopped to pull a few. An hour later, she was too hot and sweaty to go to the store so she walked out to the mailbox to get the mail. She saw some bills so took them to her office, only to see the piles all over her desk. She saw it was almost time to fix supper and could only bemoan the fact that she hadn't gotten anything accomplished all day. She was busy, but not productive.

So how do you overcome the urge to accomplish something relatively unimportant just because it feels important in the moment? *Focus, stop and breathe, and establish what really needs to get done. Then do it.*

- Forgetting where you put something when you took it off and blaming your spouse for moving it.

  My husband asked me where I'd put his shoes he'd recently worn. I told him I hadn't touched them or even seen them. I asked where he last had them, and he said right before he took a shower. I told him to check the bathroom, so he walked back into the bathroom and lo and behold, there they were! I don't know what he'd do if I weren't there to blame or accuse of moving his things—he'd have to mutter to himself until he came across them again.

- Losing our train of thought.
- Having a hard time remembering someone's name.

  I went to introduce a dear friend I've known many years to another person, and found my mind absolutely blank on her name. Talk about embarrassment. I finally said, "Tell her your name since I've lost it somewhere in my brain cells, sorry!"

- Can't think of a specific word to describe something.

  I try to get inventive and come up with all kinds of similar words until I hit on the right one.

Physical Challenges

- Stiff joints as we try to get out of bed or a chair.

  We seem to have lost our spring and flexibility and we moan and groan as we lift our weight up and out, which can be a real job if we weigh a lot. Do you know they now have a mechanism that lifts and tilts you out of a chair? Might help eliminate some of those moans and groans that escape our lips as we try to get the joints flexing again.
- Getting winded more easily.
- Having more digestive issues.

  Foods no longer agree with *you*—even if you still want them. (I've changed over to the paleo diet where you eat meat, vegetables, fruits, seeds, and nuts and have eliminated almost every one of my digestive issues.)
- Can't lose weight and get to the point you don't really care if you do or don't.

I guess I don't so much mind being old, as I mind being fat and old.
  —Benjamin Franklin

- Heart starts acting up *even when* there's no attractive person of the opposite sex around.
- No longer get excited when there *is* an attractive person of the opposite sex around.
- You get bum knees or hips and have to hobble around.

  It seems torn meniscus and chondroitis and synovitis (inflammation) is a common occurrence in people, no

matter your age. It just makes your limp more pronounced if you are "maturing."
- Your teeth may no longer be your own real ones—thank goodness mine are still my own!
- You deal with respiratory problems—shortness of breath when you walk fast.
- We get wrinkles, *lots* of wrinkles.

Please don't retouch my wrinkles. It took me so long to earn them.
—Anna Magnani

- We lose our muscle tone and strength—and our arms, bellies, and rear ends start drooping.
- We don't worry about our hair because there's not much to worry about—it seems to keep falling out.
- Things no longer work as well in the lower half.
- Can't hear clearly what other people are saying and have to ask them to repeat.
- Getting to sleep or staying asleep becomes an issue.
- Some people have to spend half their day taking pills—well, maybe a third of the day.
- Must get up lots of times at night.

I don't need you to remind me of my age. I have a bladder to do that for me.
—Stephen Fry

Energy and Motivation

- Some of us are no longer "sharp as a tack."
- Feel happy when grandkids go home so you can take a nap and have some peace and quiet. (I think this is how Gene feels when I go on my trips!)

- Exercise is something we would rather watch someone else do.

  Just look at the millions of people sitting around watching sports on TV instead of getting out to exercise themselves. I have to chuckle though when I see how many football players carry quite a bit of padding around, and it's not their gear! Maybe that's to help buffer the impact of the blows they take—maybe I could use that as my reason for my padding—to help if I fall.
- We aren't as stressed anymore because we're too tired to deal with an issue or don't care about it as much.
- Find ourselves unable to adequately take care of lawn mowing, picking up branches, or pulling out weeds in a couple of hours. It's more like a couple of days!
- Wanting to take a nap every day.

  When you are up until 1:30 or 2:00 a.m., naturally you need a nap—what is wrong with that? Or if you have to get up at 5:00 or 6:00 a.m., you need to make up for those lost hours. Naps are wonderful!

Emotional, Social, and Financial Challenges

- Having more month than money and often don't have money for the necessary things in life—like food, heating oil, essential oils, medicines, etc. I'm finding my social security check does not stretch very far.
- Feel disconnected from family and friends as kids and grandkids start families and perhaps even move away; parents and friends die and leave a void; our adult kids get so busy with their own lives they don't connect often or at all.
- Feel disconnected in our faith, especially if we no longer participate as much in church or church activities.

- We find we have times of irritation and grouchiness, and we just want to be left alone.
- We may not want to change the habits that comfort us—even if they drive other people crazy.
- Plus, many more issues that come up in individual situations.

Benefits of Aging

Benefits? Really? Just so you don't think it's all downhill as you get older, there *is* an upside to the fourth quarter of life. In fact, I'd encourage you to look at the following list as suggestions for how to be more productive at this stage of life, and not just benefits that you can take or leave.

- Cook less. I no longer have to cook every day since my husband and I normally eat twice a day, and we can be happy with fruit, simple meat, and veggie—this is one benefit I *really* like!
- Take time to go on vacations when you like without having to arrange for it at work.
- Stay wherever you are as long as you like.
- Volunteer to rock babies in hospital nurseries, or work at a school one day a week to help the teacher with kids who need attention and help they don't get at home.
- Visit in nursing homes with people who don't have any family to care about or for them.
- Volunteer at church with needed projects.
- Finally get rid of all the extra things you have accumulated in life that just take up space and collect dust. Let someone else buy them and enjoy them.

- Make space in your life and home. Save your kids from having to deal with all your "stuff" when you die.
- Spend more time with those who mean the most to you—life can be short at this point.
- Get involved with something you are really passionate about that adds meaning and enjoyment to your life.
- Open your heart to things you were afraid to try or closed off to before because family or friends discouraged you to attempt them.
- Get to know people you were taught to distrust or hate.
- Make a bucket list and start fulfilling your dreams by actually doing them.
- Make friends with neighbors, a widow/widower, a newly divorced spouse, a single parent, someone from another country who is struggling to adapt to our ways.
- Feel free to minister to people in the way God equips you and do it unashamedly and freely.
- Ask God to open your eyes and heart to what is happening around you in your own area of influence and show you how you can be used.

Life has got to be lived, that's all there is to it. At seventy, I would say the advantage is that you take life more calmly. You know that "this, too, shall pass"!
—Eleanor Roosevelt

The Power of Words and Thoughts

A major struggle many people have in this fourth quarter of life is controlling what they say and think. The "grouchy old man" or "crazy, angry old lady" stereotypes come from somewhere. Unfortunately, many elderly people exhibit the anger and grouchiness and negative words that feed these stereotypes. While some of these characteristics may result from physical pain and suffering, often people who maintain a negative attitude simply are unhappy and they let everyone know it.

I have to admit something to you: one of the biggest challenges I have had to overcome, especially in my older years, is what I say, and the *way* I say it, and what I think. I have struggled in the past, and even at times now, with being critical, negative, and judgmental of others. I have been preachy and a bit self-righteous. As I have asked God to "create in me a clean heart," I have over time found it easier to be more lenient and loving of my husband, family members, and friends. Somehow, it's easier now to see things from their perspective instead of only from my own selfish, self-centered way of looking at things.

One of my earlier coaches, Larry Beacham, encouraged me to read the book *What to Say When You Talk to Yourself* by Dr. Shad Helmstetter. This helped me see and understand that our bodies and minds respond to what we say, positively or negatively, and will give us what we ask for. So we must learn to be careful with the words that come out of our mouths. If we label ourselves as stupid, dumb, fat, ugly, ignorant, worthless, a failure, etc., that is how we will act—because we've told our subconscious how to act. Then we wonder why we feel that way or let others call us those names. Why not focus on using positive words about ourselves consistently and see if it doesn't make a difference in how we perceive and think about ourselves.

The power of what we say is one of life's greatest mysteries. Everything we do or accomplish hinges on how we choose to govern what comes out of our mouths. We can either bless our life with success and happiness or curse it into areas of sadness, failure, and discontentment.

What comes out of our mouths starts with what we think. What do we allow our minds to focus on or think about? What do *you* find yourself focusing on—the problems, the irritations from others, the list of things to do, the critical words someone said to you, the unintended snub you feel from friends or acquaintances, the loop of hurts from your past, your insecurities, your financial situation, the treatment you get from your boss and coworkers? These are just a few of the many negatives we can dwell or focus on and then find ourselves headed into a downward spiral.

> *For as he thinks in his heart, so is he.*
> —Proverbs 23:7 NKJV

> *Guard your heart above all else, for it determines the course of your life.*
> —Proverbs 4:23 NLT

> *"For whatever is in your heart determines what you say. A good person produces good things from the treasury of a good heart, and an evil person produces evil things from the treasury of an evil heart."*
> —Matthew 12:34–35 NLT

We need to recognize that *what goes on in our outer lives is a direct result of what is going on inside.* Our thoughts influence our choices and words, and as a result, influence what happens on the outside.

So we have to acknowledge that we are responsible for how our lives are going. If we don't like where we are or are headed, we need to change our thinking. Really take a look at your thought life—is it focusing on the positive or always on the negative outcomes? Do you wonder why there always seems to be a black cloud hanging over you and not others?

Our words and thoughts have energy and frequency. *Everything* has frequency and energy. If you put out negative energy, you will draw or attract to yourself negative experiences, people, and reactions. Put out positive energy, and you will attract and draw to yourself positive things. If you haven't heard about quantum physics, which deals with the energy of things and not just the chemical/physical aspects, then this may sound like a lot of "hooey" to you, but we are wonderfully and fearfully made. There is much more to us than we know or recognize. Let yourself consider that there may be more to this world than you know or understand right now, and start learning about this kind of thinking.

If you need a guideline on *what* to think about, you can't beat these words: "Fix your thoughts on what is true, and honorable, and right, and pure, and lovely, and admirable. Think about things that are excellent and worthy of praise" (Philippians 4:8 NLT).

Our thoughts are more powerful than we conceive. If you don't want to be controlled by your circumstances, then you must control what you are thinking. Otherwise you will be tossed about by life's storms and feel out of control in your life. To change situations on the outside of your life, change what is going on in your mind and heart.

Even as we age, we still need a vision, a goal, a focus of where we want to go, or what we want to achieve or experience. If you don't have a goal to work toward, you are just drifting aimlessly about in life and really . . . going nowhere. You won't know you are knocked off course when a storm throws you off track if you don't have a point or goal to realign to. So dare to dream of something you'd like to accomplish, or make, or invent, or change to help mankind. Dare to think big! We are so used to thinking of just the next day, or even the next five minutes. Lift up your eyes and look toward the horizon to see where you might aim to go. Even if you are in the last quarter of life with me, we all still need to have a purpose to work toward, a reason to get up that energizes us.

Some things that drive me to get up and out every day are these:

- I desire to build up my team in our business, so they can see and have success in their lives.

- I desire to make enough money monthly to be able to support four missionary families that are dear to me.
- I desire to speak to groups about how they can have as much optimal health as possible, no matter where they are in age or current health situation.
- I desire to give people a blueprint or guide to help them find defining moments that have impacted the course of their lives, so they can find their gift to share with others.
- I desire to meet more people and impact their lives with what I have to offer of myself—the knowledge I've gained and the help I give with the tools I use.

I've found that as we get older, not only does our physical body change, and give us many challenges, but our emotional and spiritual aspects are impacted as well. Now I want to look at each area of "us" and see how we might cope with all the changes that take place.

Chapter 8
Spirit: Our First Aspect of "Being"

As we examine areas of our lives that are impacted as we age, we need to look beyond just the physical. As we talk about our lives, who we are, and what we have accomplished, we need to look deeper and address our whole being—*spirit, soul, and body*. We aren't made up of just what we can see, feel, and touch. That's simply the exterior, the vessel that contains our *real* essence.

We are made up of three parts—spirit, soul, and body. Actually we find many examples in the Bible, nature, history, culture, and literature of objects or concepts having three parts:

- egg shell, egg white, and egg yolk
- liquid water, steam, and ice
- germ layers: endoderm, mesoderm, ectoderm
- gold, frankincense, and myrrh
- Abraham, Isaac, and Jacob
- the truth, the whole truth, and nothing but the truth
- of the people, by the people, for the people
- hear no evil, see no evil, speak no evil
- faith, hope, and charity
- Father, Son, and Holy Spirit

- rock, paper, scissors
- Peter, Paul, and Mary
- *Wynken, Blynken, and Nod*
- snap, crackle, and pop
- *The Good, the Bad, and the Ugly*
- small, medium, and large
- Ready, aim, fire!
- On your mark, get set, go!

Okay, you get the point—threes abound! Can you think of any more to add to the list? It seems natural for things to come in sets of three. It's even said that troubles come that way.

The part of our being mentioned first in the Bible is the *spirit*, which is the part of us that connects to God. I must admit I always thought *body, soul, and spirit* was the correct order. So as I prepared for a class on how essential oils impact every area of our being, I looked up the reference in the Bible where it mentions a different order. It's found in 1 Thessalonians 5:23: "Now may the God of peace Himself sanctify you completely; and may your whole *spirit, soul, and body* be preserved blameless at the coming of our Lord Jesus Christ" (NKJV, emphasis mine).

It jolted me to see the body wasn't mentioned first. That's the way we always talk about the order and the part we emphasize the most. Just look at all of today's marketing to see what advertisers and companies are selling—clothes, makeup, weight loss, hair products—how we look. Culture talks about the body so much (even using it to sell items like cars), it's no wonder we tend to think of it first in the three areas of our being. Since the Bible mentions the spirit first, it must be of more importance, and the body is listed last—contrary to the world's view of "being." So we will discuss this first and primary aspect of being in terms of living our fourth quarter in life.

Chapter 8

My Spiritual Being

In the days when we were active in our first church in Florida, I felt very much on fire in my relationship with God and so close to Him as I learned, taught classes, and led the Prayer Closet at church. I never thought I'd fall off that spiritual level, until we went through the "divorce" as we left that church and began our search for another one.

That experience took me through many levels of disappointment with leadership, feeling bereft of comfort, loneliness, feeling adrift, and being estranged from everyone I knew and loved in our former church. As you can see, I had a hard time accepting change and just rolling with the punches. I had a hard time praying, reading God's Word, and talking about what God was doing in my life—it was so painful I really *couldn't* see what God was doing.

As time passed, and I achieved some distance and perspective on the whole situation, I could see how God was drawing and using me outside of the setting of the church. I realized how He allowed me to be taken away from all I felt comfortable with and relied on in order to get my complete attention on Him—not on all I was doing to serve Him. I had to see how poor in spirit I was without Him as my primary focal point.

When I was taken out of that comfort zone, I was finally in a place where He could expose me to mission trips. My mind and heart had to be free of responsibilities and being in leadership roles where I was focused on what I was *doing*. I needed to focus on *being* what He was calling me to *be*. I've often heard this saying: "We are human beings, not human doings." We must *be* before we can *do*. And what we *do* should come out of *who we are*, not the other way around.

So how can we *be*, instead of *do*? To be is not to just sit around like a lump and not interact with life. Here are some of the "be's" I realized I must pursue in my own life:

- I must *be willing* to see I am sinful and in need of someone to save me from the consequences of my sin.
- I must *be sold out* to letting Him be the Lord and Master of my life.
- I must *be willing to change*, and *be consecrated* to living as He would have me live (the directions are in the Manufacturer's Handbook—the Bible).
- I must *be open* to correction, discipline and *being taught*.
- I must *be still* and know that He is God and I am not.
- I must *be in relationship* with Him.

I am not trying to sound sanctimonious with all these words as I am far from being a Goody Two-shoes. I just know this list describes the things I need in my own life when I consider the spiritual aspect of life. And I'm sure I could add many more.

"Being Still"

I found some interesting thoughts written by Fritz Chery on the website BibleReasons when I Googled the phrase *being still*:

> There's just too much noise! There's just too much movement! Have you ever wondered how some Christians can be going through the worst pain and suffering and still they have joy? It's because they are being still. They put all their worries in God's hands.
>
> We need to listen to God's quiet voice that comes to us in our mind and heart rather than focusing on the things

that are concerning us. Let your joy come from knowing you are God's child and held in His arms. Circumstances can always change, but He never does.

He has already proved that He can calm any storm. Sometimes God allows trials so you can learn to be more dependent on Him. God is saying, "I'm in control. I can do all things. Stop fearing and trust in me instead." When your thoughts are running rampant, don't seek temporary help by watching TV, going on the internet, etc.[5]

Personally, I have a hard time just being still, but that is what we need to do to get away from the clamor of the world so we can hear from God. Do you struggle with this—to get quiet enough to hear from God to let His peace steal over you as you submit yourself and your problems to Him?

Be still in God. Learn to relax in His presence. Find places where you can experience a calming environment and then listen for His voice, even in the silence. If you struggle with understanding how much He loves you and wants to care for you, take the time to remember. Recall how He's helped you in the past, and others, and even those in the Bible. He promises us He'll never leave us or forsake us. When you take time to be still, you will sense His calming voice and His strength. Be still, know He is God, and let Him guide you.

Many people feel they don't need to go to church—instead they say they need weekend time to rest from their week of work, or get things done. I personally think when we miss church, we miss a time of coming away from the noise of the world to hear from the Word of the Lord and lift up our voices in praise to Him. I know that in Hebrews 10:25 we are told not to forsake the gathering together of believers as we need the fellowship and we minister to one another with our gifts. However, we need to not depend *only* on church to be our *primary* contact with God—we need a personal relationship with Him that goes with us everywhere.

So many people simply practice and worship "religion." That focuses on rules, regulations, and traditional practices—which are man-inspired. Mere "religion" feels empty and shallow, like you are going through the motions week after week. I got to the point where I had a hard time going to church just to make people think I was being "good" and practicing my faith. I wanted to find a church where the people assembled as the body of Christ and the focus was on worshiping God and seeing that He got the attention and glory. His Word was our focus because we wanted to hear from Him.

It took a lot of searching and visiting different churches to find a place where we felt the presence of the Holy Spirit and that the believers who gathered there welcomed us as a necessary part they had been missing.

I still find I hold back from getting fully involved in all the church's activities because some of it feels like just busyness. I want to take my faith out into the marketplace where I meet people on a one-on-one basis and integrate my faith into my business life. I want my relationship with God to exude from me so that people know there's something different about me that makes me trustworthy, dependable, and willing to do my best for them because of *whose* I am.

Evaluate Your Spiritual Aspect

We change in many ways through our lifetime, and our spiritual relationship is one of them. You may have grown much closer to God through life's tragedies, *or* fallen completely away from that close and personal relationship because of tragedies and blaming God. Through my circumstances, I learned it's all about *relationship* with our maker and creator—God—and not *religion,* which blindly follows traditions made by man and diverts our attention and affection from the living God.

It seems much easier to follow God when we are young and have been instructed by church and parents to do so, but when we get out on our own, we get diverted by the world around us, education, careers, desire to make money, and enjoying all the pleasures that lie before us. We may get too busy to feed our spiritual nature by reading His Word and talking to Him. I am as guilty as anyone else in being too busy for the spiritual priorities, so they get pushed aside to be done later. But we *need* this time of communication with Him to get our direction and guidance for the day.

I believe God when He says a judgment day is coming, and how we choose to live our life down here on this testing ground determines where we spend eternity. If we live our lives aimlessly, without the goal of heaven in mind, we will be tossed to and fro with the circumstances of our lives. If you get knocked down, it's easier when you have a spiritual relationship with God to get your bearings again and get pointed in the right direction.

I *know* I need this foundation in my life, and without it I am totally adrift. On my wall, I have a plaque that reads:

Life, the time God gives us to choose how you spend eternity.

As we, each one of us, are getting closer to meeting our maker, we need to take time to evaluate where we are in our walk with Christ. If changes need to be made, *now* is the time—before it's too late.

Sometimes we forget that we can be one auto accident, one step out in traffic, one heart attack, one stroke, one bullet, one freak accident away from dying. We may not have many more days or years to make a choice or decision to change our direction to accept

Christ as our Savior. We may enjoy our sinning too much to want to change. Maybe we should realize we are playing Russian roulette with our lives, and the eternal results can be deadly.

I encourage you to evaluate your spiritual status in this fourth quarter of life. Have you become stagnant in your relationship with the One who loves you more than anyone else can? Has God slipped off your radar and you're just living your life as you see fit? Are you just going through the motions of being a "Christian" and think you are okay because you fulfill the requirements of church membership? You could ask yourself a lot of questions, but a telling one is this: Do you feel full or empty in your spirit? What does this introspection make you want to do?

This is *your final quarter.* Are you living each day as though that fact applies to you? Are you willing to do the hard work of evaluating where you really are in your life? Are you willing to see that many of the things we do are just time wasters and could be applied to better serving others rather than just ourselves? Are you willing to stop and lay aside practices that lead you into sin rather than into a closer walk with the Lord? Are you willing to share your money to help others who are struggling with the heavy load life puts them under?

This can be a *really* hard thing for most of us, as we like to hang onto all our worldly pleasures, but these pleasures are temporary, fleeting, and not really satisfying in the end. What is satisfying is a close, intimate walk with the Lord and knowing He is guiding our steps, opening doors for service, and nudging us when we get off the right path. I want His guidance, correction, and instruction. I want His discipline because that shows me I am His child and He cares enough to correct me.

How about you? Where are you in this spiritual walk? Do you know that what is going on inside us spiritually impacts how we are physically and emotionally? We need to look at that next.

Chapter 9
Soul—Emotional and Mental Mind-sets: Our Second Aspect of "Being"

Getting old ain't for sissies.
—Bette Davis

Facing the aspect of getting older is not for wimps; it can be tough! As our bodies progress through many physical changes, we may not be the emotional person we used to be. We face despair, loss of feeling needed and important to others, being set aside as though we are in the way, health issues that can be incapacitating and make us dependent on others, loss of income and increasing health-care expenses, and depression as we see our life coming to its end. Some may be ready for the end; others are fighting it tooth and nail.

Our Mental State

The fourth quarter of life may bring loneliness and depression, as well as excessive drinking for some elderly people, which can lead to falls, forgetfulness, and dementia. Some have lost a spouse and are now alone, which brings fear and anxiety. Many in these later years of life lose hope and feel nothing is left except the end, and that brings fear.

Depression may set in as fear increases, and for many in the last quarter of life, one of the greatest fears is a diminished mental capacity. Even the simplest sign of forgetfulness, like losing one's keys or glasses, can be enough to convince some people that they have dementia or even Alzheimer's disease. While incidences of these mental changes do increase with age, a fear of even the *possibility* of such a diagnosis will send many into further isolation. And this, according to some experts, may increase the likelihood of a diminished mental state.

When people have few close personal relationships to keep them from feeling lonely, they have more inclination for dementia, as there's no one to keep them focused and active mentally.

Professor Tara Spires-Jones, a dementia expert at Edinburgh University, said:

> The science behind a potential link between relationships and reduced dementia risk is fascinating. . . . Humans are social animals, and maintaining close relationships, like marriage, is likely to keep our brains active and healthy.
> You can be surrounded by people, but it is the number of *close* relationships that is associated with a reduced risk for dementia . . . it's not about the quantity.[6]

An article by Dr. Joseph Mercola emphasized the increase in mental health problems in our country, and the issues that come with a proliferation of psychotropic medications.

America Struggles with Notable Decline in Mental Health

While prescriptions for psychiatric drugs keep increasing (when you include other drugs beside antidepressants, such as anti-anxiety drugs, nearly 17 percent of American adults are medicated), several parameters show mental health in the U.S. is declining.

Suicide rates are at a 30-year high, mental disorders are now the second most common cause of disability, having risen sharply since 1980, and prescription drug abuse and overdose deaths have become a public health emergency. While opioid painkillers are among the most lethal, psychiatric drugs also take their toll. In 2013, anti-anxiety benzodiazepine drugs accounted for nearly one-third of prescription overdose deaths.

These statistics suggest that far from being helpful, antidepressants and other psychiatric drugs are making the situation worse. Sure, these drugs may be helpful for a small minority of people with very severe mental health problems, such as schizophrenia, but clearly, the clear majority of people using these drugs do not suffer from severe psychiatric illness.

Most are struggling with sadness, grief, anxiety, "the blues," and depression, which are in many ways part of your body's communication system, revealing nutritional or sunlight deficiencies and/or spiritual disconnect, for example. The underlying reasons for these kinds of troubles are manifold, but you can be sure that, whatever the cause, an antidepressant will not correct it.[7]

Many older people have little to no money to live on, poor housing situations, and no support system or family to care for them.

So if you look at aging from the aspect of a loneliness or isolation, this time of life can feel bleak and depressing. The whole situation of living seems grim, distressing, gloomy and joyless.

The Final Quarter

Thinking of how little they have to exist on, how little they have to eat, how they can't afford medications or doctor visits to deal with their health issues, how they have no one to count on or love them—all of these manifestations of poverty make people feel as if life is helpless and hopeless. It's an understandable mind-set and emotional quagmire. There doesn't seem to be any light to brighten their days.

However, in my own situation, I choose to see this part of my life as a time of freedom, especially as I still have my health, husband, family, and home. I am blessed beyond measure, and I choose to not throw away the chances I have to bloom and to explore all I can do and be.

We now have time to work on relationships with our significant others, where before we were tied up with business and making a living, taking care of family needs, and activities. We may even feel guilt at spending so much time "taking care of business" in the past that we've forgotten to stop along the way to smell the roses and appreciate the smallest things in life. Now we have a chance to do so.

Are you willing to keep exploring—if not physically, then mentally—and stay sharp and present in the moment? Even if you have health issues that keep you more homebound, you can explore new ideas, new hobbies, or new interests. Do you read, do puzzles or Sudoku, play cards, or listen to beautiful music that transports you to greater heights? In whatever way possible, find opportunities to explore the world, learn something new, even meet new people. The pursuit of new knowledge and relationships will not only keep you from loneliness and an increased depressed emotional state but also could keep your mind sharper longer.

Are you open to doing things in another way rather than being stuck in your rut of "doing it my way"? Maybe your way served you for many years, but you may also have missed the joy of doing something new and different. Don't be a stick in the mud! Open your mind and let the moths out, as they may have been nibbling away and eating your dreams and robbing you of a more fulfilling life.

Are you determined to go to the grave still "doing it my way"? Or are you open to the idea that life still has more to offer you, and you still have the capacity to learn and grow and enjoy life to its fullest?

Feeding Your Soul

What *can* you do at the age of seventy-five, or *whatever* age you are now, to feed your soul, to improve your mental and emotional mind-sets?

Let me throw some suggestions and thoughts your way. I have become more alive and mentally active now that I have the freedom to try new things, like starting a business, utilizing social media, going out and meeting new people in networking groups, learning from others who are experts in their niche, and putting it all into practice.

If you have had an active and meaningful life, why not write a book, and share your wisdom and experiences with others? What do you think I am doing?

Be willing to let others coach, guide, and teach you in some new endeavor. Who said we must retire? That word is not even in the Bible, and *that's* my operating manual. Don't be the walking dead—live until the day you die!

Change your mind-set, release any negative emotional hurts and experiences you hold on to that keep you tied down. Perhaps you reacted poorly in situations by losing your temper, reacting with anger or violence, sulking, or withdrawing and then justified those reactions because of what happened to you in the past. Those reactions have become your way of dealing with hard or trying situations. Rather than seeking to grow past those ingrained patterns and learn how to handle them in a positive way, we hang on to ways that no longer serve us in a healthy manner. Let the past be the past—you live in the present with the future ahead, so let go of that ball and chain. Christ died so we could be free and be "new creations." You spit in His face by refusing to let go of the sins and failures of what happened in your past. He forgave you; forgive yourself.

If you are God's child and a part of His family, you have a future, an inheritance, and eternity with Him. That's something to hang your hat on and be joyful about.

We could talk on and on about our past—our hurts, humiliations, disappointments, disasters, loss of loved ones, missed opportunities, feelings of being overlooked or let down. But why rehash all the old stuff—let it go and face forward for what lies ahead.

> *When our emotional health is in a bad state, so is our level of self-esteem. We have to slow down and deal with what is troubling us, so that we can enjoy the simple joy of being happy and at peace with ourselves.*
> —Jess C. Scott

Emotional traumas that happen when we are young can follow us through life. Remember that ten-year-old girl who was messed up when she fell and broke her teeth through her lip, talked with a lisp at times, who had chipped teeth as well as a Dutch-boy haircut, who avoided people, and read to escape? My past influenced my perception of myself for decades, and made me feel like I was still an ugly little girl. I have struggled with being able to accept compliments, being able to think of myself as acceptable to others or even pretty.

I have finally come face-to-face with the fact that my perception was just that—a perception—and have now been able to let go of that young girl. It took someone shining a light on the situation to help me face what had been going on all those years. I feel like a butterfly that has finally come out of the cocoon, and I'm now able to fly! That box I had erected around myself to protect and hide me is no longer needed. I'm ready to shine!

Running a marathon with a backpack is tough and may hinder you from winning the race. Don't let the baggage from your past—heavy with fear, guilt, and anger—slow you down.
—Maddy Malhotra

We are coming down to the wire in this race called *life*, so let's shine as we get to the end.

- Smile when you see people—it lights you up!
- Give a cheerful word to encourage someone.
- Share your wealth now—it won't do you any good in the grave. Let your kids earn their own way; you did.
- Read some great books that can transport you into others' lives, places, and cultures. If you can't read any longer, listen to audiotapes. You can get them so cheaply from the library.
- Reach out to a hurting friend, take them out to eat or for coffee, and give them a supportive shoulder to cry on if that's what's needed.
- Go over and meet the neighbors that you've driven past for the last twenty years. They might end up being good friends.

- Take your family on vacations they can't afford themselves if you have the means to do so. Make memories with them that they can look back on when you are gone.

I have three sisters, and we try to get together every year for a sisters' vacation. Of course, our husbands come too as they don't want to miss all the fun we girls have. We laugh our heads off at silly things said or done until our bellies hurt from all the laughing. Ann's husband sneakily takes videos of us and then posts them on Facebook, trying to embarrass us. We have taught each other the classes we prepared for our own business teams, given each other massages; tried out clay masks and then laughed so hard at each other we made our "faces" crack, had ionic foot baths, and the list goes on.

We share hurts, pains, concerns for family, and rejoice when good things happen. We know we are there for each other until we all go home to be with our eternal family. I treasure these special times when we all set aside time to meet up together.

Does this trigger any thoughts in your own mind of things you can change, or add to enrich your life? Can you think of ways to have more impact on your family, and if you don't have a family, then your friends or people around you? I encourage you to make at least one change a week, or month. Do it for twenty-one days to make it a habit, and see if it makes you feel better, lifts that sense of depression, puts more spring in your step, and gives you a sense of anticipation every morning as to what the day holds. Just *do it*!

Appreciate the Little Things

My sister Pat sent me an article that expressed a thought that could be relevant to each of us living our fourth quarter, or really, anyone.

Lisa Beamer, the wife of Todd Beamer—famous for shouting, "Let's roll!" before he and fellow passengers overcame the terrorists attempting to fly their plane to Washington, DC—appeared on *Good Morning America*. In her interview she talked about the little things she missed most about Todd, like hearing the garage door open as he came home, and her children running to meet him.

Lisa said she had learned to appreciate life in spite of her loss. In so doing, she recalled the story of a special teacher she had in high school many years ago whose husband died suddenly of a heart attack. About a week after his death, Lisa recalled, here's what that teacher shared with her classroom of students:

> As the late afternoon sunlight came streaming in through the classroom windows and the class was nearly over, she moved a few things aside on the edge of her desk and sat down there. With a gentle look of reflection on her face, she paused and said, "Class is over. I would like to share with all of you a thought that is unrelated to class, but which I feel is very important. Each of us is put here on earth to learn, share, love, appreciate and give of ourselves. None of us knows when this fantastic experience will end. It can be taken away at any moment.
>
> "Perhaps this is God's way of telling us that we must make the most out of every single day." Her eyes were beginning to water, but she went on, "So I would like you all to make me a promise. From now on, on your way to school, or on your way home, find something beautiful to notice.
>
> "It doesn't have to be something you see; it could be a scent, perhaps of freshly baked bread wafting out of someone's house, or it could be the sound of the breeze slightly rustling the leaves in the trees, or the way the morning light catches one autumn leaf as it falls gently to the ground. Please look for these things, and cherish them.

For, although it may sound trite to some, these things are the 'stuff' of life. The little things we are put here on earth to enjoy. The things we often take for granted."

After the teacher spoke, Lisa remembered, she and her classmates were totally quiet. They picked up their papers and books and left the room silently. That afternoon, Lisa began to notice the little things a lot more every day. She is grateful especially for being able to appreciate the little things about her husband. She reminded the viewers to notice something special at lunch, to walk on the grass barefoot, to eat ice cream, because the older we get, we won't regret what we did, but what we didn't do.[8]

> *Too often we underestimate the power of a touch, a smile, a kind word, a listening ear, an honest compliment, or the smallest act of caring, all of which have the potential to turn a life around.*
> —Leo Buscaglia

As you consider this last quarter of life, be intentional about creating a positive mental and emotional mind-set. Find ways to engage with the world, with people, and with God. When your soul is healthy, you will have more peace and joy, and you'll be able to share that with others. Be God's hands to others—reach out in love. You can impact someone in a way you may never realize. When you get to heaven, there may be a line of people waiting to thank you for the impact you had on their lives. Glory!

> *It's sad to grow old, but nice to ripen.*
> —Brigitte Bardot

Chapter 10
Body: Our Third Aspect of "Being"

Our body may be the last of the parts mentioned in that passage from the Bible, but it *is* the part that holds the rest of us together, so you might want to take good care of it. What takes place in our bodies as we age? Does it happen overnight, or has it been changing all through the years and we just haven't noticed? For me, it was as if I didn't really want to see the age spots or the gray hair, the wrinkles and jowl developing, until I was forced to take a good look when I turned seventy. Then it was like, "Who is this older lady?"

I still don't feel "old," as I have so much energy; so much desire to go places and work with people, do things that tax my body, keep learning, go to network meetings, and connect with other interesting people. So doesn't that mean I'm still young—if only in my mind? I think our minds have a lot to do with how old we feel or act. So I plan to stay mentally active, interested, and turned on by people, things, and places so I can continue to come across as still young. Doesn't this sound like where you'd like to be too?

Health is a state of complete physical, mental, and social well-being, and not merely the absence of disease or infirmity.
—World Health Organization

The Final Quarter

I read with amazement of how many Old Testament biblical people lived to very ripe ages:

Genesis 5:5—Adam died at 930 years of age. (*Torah table.)
Genesis 5:8—Seth died at 912 years of age.
Genesis 5:11—Enosh died at 905 years of age.
Genesis 5:14—Kenan died at 910 years of age.
Genesis 5:17—Mahalalel died at 895 years of age.
Genesis 5:20—Yered died at 962 years of age.
Genesis 5:23—Enoch died at 365 years of age.
Genesis 5:27—Methuselah died at 969 years of age (oldest)
Genesis 5:31—Lamech died at 777 years of age.
Noah died at 950 years of age.
Shem died at 600 years of age.
Terach died at 205 years of age.
Abraham died at 175 years of age.
Isaac died at 180 years of age.
Jacob died at 147 years of age.
Moses died at 120 years of age.

I often wonder how their bodies held up for that length of time. We reach our sixties, seventies, and on up and just look at what happens to us. We get wrinkles, lose our muscle tone, develop joint problems, lose sight; our hearing diminishes, strength lessens, minds get lost somewhere, hormones go haywire—every aspect of our being seems to be deteriorating, but it doesn't have to be that way.

Look at our life expectancy in this day and age: males, seventy-six; females, eighty-one. What a difference from those biblical examples. Ever wonder why this is so? What has changed in our world—besides everything?

Chapter 10

We now take in chemicals in every aspect of life:

- We eat processed, chemical-laden foods.
- Even real foods are nutritionally deficient.
- We drink everything except water.
- We take more drugs than were even heard or thought of back in biblical days.
- We put chemicals on every part of our bodies.
- We sit and walk on chemical-loaded furniture and carpets/flooring.
- We put chemicals around our homes to kill bugs.
- We breathe in fumes loaded with chemicals.
- We inject them into our bodies with vaccines.
- We put them on our teeth . . .

. . . and then we wonder *what has gone wrong?*

We need to start thinking of our health in a deeper way than just managing our symptoms. Why are we feeling them? Is there a deficiency in our cell health that has gone on so long that it's now affecting the whole system?

Why not think about nourishing our bodies from the cellular level out, instead of just trying to suppress the symptoms? Are we starving our bodies by withholding the tools it needs to heal itself? How long has it been since you've eaten healthy, whole, organic, unprocessed foods? Are you supplementing your diet with healthy fats, food enzymes, anti-oxidant drinks, healthy proteins, and lots of clean water?

Well, a good majority of us take the easy way out in taking care of our hunger and eat whatever is prepared for us—stopping at the grocery store, fast-food place, or restaurant. We have no idea what has been put in or on the foods we eat, so we take in more chemicals than we know. We get loaded up with high fructose corn syrup, GMO foods, hormone/antibiotic-laden meats, and nutritionally depleted processed foods.

Then we wonder why we get sick so often or catch whatever is going around the office, school, or workplace. Our bodies don't have the ammunition to deal with invaders. Our immune systems are running low; we are stressed, have trouble sleeping, and have poor fuel with which to power our bodies.

What's the answer? I can't even begin to deal with every symptom we experience as we age, but we can talk about how our bodies are often greatly impacted as the years accumulate.

Supporting a Healthier Body

Our structural system—bones, muscles, ligaments—is crucial for our physical movement and support, which we need to maintain as we age, so we *really* must keep moving and exercise. Muscle aches and joint pains are quite common as we age, but it's probably caused more by *lack* of exercise. Our bodies are designed to move rather than sitting for hours on end. Unfortunately, we have become more sedentary the older we get, as we turn to TV, computers, cell phones, iPads, etc. to entertain us and help us work. All we have to do is push a button to get things done.

Many of our health issues increase because of this move from living and working outside to living in our chairs in front of a desk for hours at a time. We see more heart disease, depression, cancers, high blood pressure, obesity, and sleep issues.

Natural Pain Relievers and Anti-Inflammatory Supplements

We can find many natural supplements to deal with all our health issues. These are healthier for our bodies, and have less chance of causing harm. I would highly recommend starting at this natural level of self-care when you are still young and vital, however, it's never too late to begin healthy nutrition habits. I will tell you what I have found to be of great help just to give you some ideas of where I started.

Every day I take vitamin D3, omega 3 fats, food enzymes, probiotics, Sulfurzyme (a Young Living product that contains sulfur—needed by every cell in your body—and powdered Ningxia Red (a powerful anti-oxidant from Young Living) that enables the body to utilize the sulfur. Sulfurzyme helps with reviving our immune systems, supports almost every major bodily function, and forestalls an array of degenerative conditions. I find it to be a wonderfully effective product that also helps me maintain healthy skin, hair, and nails.

I have learned so much from Dr. Joseph Mercola's website (www.mercola.com) and the articles he writes to recommend for natural ways to deal with health issues. I am not going to go into details about them, as you can look them up for yourself.

Diet

This is the number-one thing that can help reduce inflammation in your body and help with digestion issues, allergies, weight, etc. I have changed the way I eat to twice a day with a late breakfast and early supper. That enables my body to have a fasting time from 7:00 p.m. to 9:00 or 10:00 the next morning. I have cut out dairy, cheeses, breads, pasta, lots of meat, pastries, sodas, and processed foods. So here's what I do eat: small amounts of meat, vegetables—cooked and raw—salads, fruits, nuts and seeds, eggs with organic sausages, and water to drink. I have plenty to eat and it fills me up without hunger pangs later. I admit I cheat every now and then, but find it doesn't sit as well with me when I do. I am happy with this simple food plan as I feel so much better digestive-wise. Some people call it the paleo diet—I just call it the basic foods diet!

Some other things you can use which help with digestion are: curcumin, ginger, boswellia, bromelain, and capsaicin.

I think of how life must have been tough as the people in Bible days had to grow their own crops, then harvest and prepare them to save or eat; take care of their flocks, moving them to fresh pastures over many miles and overseeing their animals' health and protection; build their homes from scratch; make their own clothes; travel by foot everywhere they went; draw their own water; cook over open fires and prepare just enough, as there was no refrigeration to preserve foods; wash clothes by hand and dry them on bushes. They ate moderately and always moved about. I'm thinking *that* was a healthier lifestyle than ours today.

Do you ever think that all our "progress" is really harming us rather than progressing us? Our diets have changed—and not for the better—with:

- nutritionally depleted soil
- genetically modified foods
- crops sprayed with pesticides and herbicides
- antibiotics added to almost everything
- synthetic additives (to enhance taste and shelf life) with negative impacts on our bodies
- foods made entirely out of chemicals
- flour/sugar/salt—everything is processed to leave it stripped of the real nutrients and then replaced with synthetics
- sodas that deplete our bodies of calcium and add lots of sugar, as well as being highly acidic
- most everything we eat has some form of high fructose corn syrup in it

- grains genetically changed to a form that is different from what our bodies were designed to handle so now we have many people with gluten sensitivities

The list goes on and on.

These are the problems we face. How can we help ourselves during this dietary fiasco?

To me, good health is more than just exercise and diet. It's really a point of view and a mental attitude you have about yourself.
—Albert Schweitzer

So what can you eat to have a healthy diet? Well, forget the recommended diet plans, as they will have you eating grains and sugars. Start by eating real food. Use meats from animals that are raised eating grass, with no hormones or antibiotics; same way with eggs—from free-range chickens given no hormones or antibiotics. Eat healthy fats, like avocados, coconut oil, nuts, seeds, and raw organic butter. Eat lots of vegetables, moderate amounts of fruits, and cut out the carbs. After eating this way for a while, you will find you don't have the cravings for breads, pastries, and pasta. You might even watch some weight slide off that "young" body of yours.

What Else Impacts Our Health?

Most of us are exposed daily to technology, without much thought of its impact on our health, only its convenience. We have become a tech-oriented society with all its attendant issues, especially a great reduction in human interaction—we'd rather talk/text on cell phones than have a face-to-face conversation. We sit for hours in front of TV, computers, or iPads and don't go outside to exercise to get fresh air and sunshine. Our minds may be sharp, but our bodies are flabby!

We can't jump off bridges anymore because our iPhones will get ruined. We can't take skinny dips in the ocean because there's no service on the beach and adventures aren't real unless they're on Instagram. Technology has doomed the spontaneity of adventure and we're helping destroy it every time we Google, check-in, and hashtag.
—Jeremy Glass

Through technology we are also exposed to great amounts of EMF, electromagnetic frequencies, which can alter our cells. Think of all the TVs, microwaves, fluorescent lights, cell phones, cell towers, wi-fi modems, computers, iPads, etc. that we are around daily.

Little kids using cell phones are shown to have increased brain cell tumors, especially on the side they put the phone to. Their skull is thinner and more easily penetrated by the EMFs. Adults can develop brain and parotid tumors.

Do you suffer from any of the following common illnesses and ailments, which have all been scientifically linked to cell-phone-information-carrying radio waves?

- Alzheimer's, senility, and dementia
- Parkinson's disease
- autism
- fatigue
- headaches
- sleep disruptions
- altered memory function, poor concentration, and spatial awareness

Chapter 10

Although cancer and brain tumors are most often cited as the potential health risks from cell phone radiation, as you can see, cancer is not the only, or the most common, danger you and your children/grandchildren face.

A way to eliminate having the radiation come directly into your brain cells is to use an air-tube headset, which conducts sound but keeps the radiation from traveling up the headset wire to your brain.

We have become a sick society, chemicals *in and on* everything, our hormones out of whack, diabetes rampant, obesity as the newest epidemic affecting so many, cancer, cardiovascular issues, kidney stones, depression, suicides, infertility, thyroid problems, kids having more problems at younger ages and then administered drugs to control them, people given drugs for every issue they mention, and the list goes on and on.

What Do We Do?

How can we address all the changes that occur as we get older? We must look at the big picture to see what is happening and what we can change to make it better for us individually.

One of the huge things that impact us all is the chemical overload we are exposed to. This is one area where we can make decisions to change that can impact our health greatly.

Rather than trying to address all the health issues we face with possible solutions and get in trouble with the FDA, I decided to share what I have done to lighten the chemical load or onslaught on my body. I use almost every one of these products to replace the chemical-laden OTC products in the stores.

When I discovered the Young Living Essential Oil Company twenty years ago, I didn't realize what a *gold mine* I had found. They produce many personal care products, skin care, makeup, and home cleaning products—all without harmful chemicals. Their essential oils are produced without chemicals and are incorporated into every one of their products to enhance their effectiveness.

Here are some of the products I've used to switch from chemical-laden to chemical-free. Starting from the outside in:

- Lavender or Copaiba shampoo and conditioner
- A.R.T. skin care
- Sassy Minerals makeup line
- deodorants
- lavender hand and body lotion
- Thieves toothpaste and mouthwash
- Thieves waterless hand sanitizer that kills bad and not good bacteria, as well as foaming hand soaps
- many different essential oils for a variety of issues and to enhance the immune systems
- Thieves laundry soap and Thieves cleaner, which kill the spores of mold and mildew
- Thieves cleaner added to loads of laundry or diluted as a spray for rooms, carpets, floors, bathrooms, pets, sprayed in AC filters, etc.
- Thieves oil diffused to freshen and clean the air, and many other uses

Every day I apply Progessence Plus as well as Endoflex essential oil to support my hormone/endocrine system, and make me a "nicer to be around" woman. Just ask my husband. I also use the oils on my face and put Sandalwood moisturizer on top of them.

For inner use (These supplements all contain top-of-the line ingredients and have essential oils added to facilitate and speed up the absorption of the ingredients; they all enhance my health.):

- Sulfurzyme
- Super B
- BLM and Agilease for bone, ligament, and muscle support
- Essentialzyme 4—food enzymes to break down the foods to get the nutrition out of them
- Life 9 probiotics
- SleepEssence, which helps on those nights I can't go to sleep by providing melatonin and four sleep-enhancing essential oils
- a Vitality line of essential oils that can be used for internal use—adding them to a drink, foods, or capsule to enhance the taste and support your overall health

When we look at how we are bombarded and saturated with chemicals, why would you *not* want to do all you can to lighten that load? Everything must go through our livers to be cleansed and broken down to a usable form after toxins are removed. If the liver is overloaded with toxins, it cannot function properly. We then start to have health issues because our liver is overworked just dealing with the chemicals/toxins.

Why not do all you can to prolong your life and improve the quality of it?

Look at everything you drink—sodas, coffees, sugar-laden Starbucks coffee drinks, energy drinks, sodas (I know, I'm repeating myself but I'm trying to make the point that sodas are bad!), teas to excess—and decide to go with what your body needs and craves—pure water!

How many processed foods are you using to replace fruits, vegetables, and lean meats that are healthier to eat? I'm not pointing fingers, as I am also guilty at times of using easy, already packaged foods to make meal preparation quicker and less of a hassle. But I know better, and am having weight issues because of *not doing* what I know to do.

Our bodies are fighting inflammation because of our diets. Inflammation is the number-one cause of many of our health issues. If we can see the progression of cause and effect, we can decide to stop the merry-go-round at some point. Hopefully it will be sooner rather than later, when it's gotten past the point of no return.

Most of us are also acidic from all we eat and drink, and the body constantly has to rob minerals from other areas to neutralize the acid. That is one reason for the increase in osteoporosis. The body will fight to stay in the 7.4 range of pH, and do whatever it has to maintain it, so it takes calcium from our bones and teeth. After years of that, our bones become porous and more brittle. We rob Peter to pay Paul.

Medications are another cause of our acidity. How many drugs do you take, and how long have you taken them? Have you considered trying to take care of issues with alternative methods? Thousands of people have regained their health by going back to nature, and saying no to drugs or being bombarded by chemotherapy and radiation.

I encourage you to find a naturopathic health doctor to help guide you into natural modalities that are more compatible with our bodies and don't cause the harm that can occur with synthetic drugs.

I'm also *not* saying to go off your medicines unless you are doing it under your doctor's monitoring, as that can be dangerous. Some drugs cannot be stopped cold without serious side effects. Hopefully you can find a doctor who is open to alternative modalities and is willing to let you incorporate them into your care.

I know you may be laughed at, derided, and maybe even called a deluded kook, but God created our bodies as well as the medicines in nature to help heal our diseases. (Read Ezekiel 47:12 and Revelation 22:2.) He made our bodies to heal themselves, so use the things that give your body the tools it needs to enable that healing process. Drugs suppress the symptoms and don't heal us. They can be loaded with side effects because of synthetic ingredients that don't fit our cell receptor sites, but have to be broken down by the liver.

Sometimes complementary medicine (using the best of both worlds) is the wisest decision—using today's medicines in times of heart attack or trauma, when baby deliveries go awry, when surgery is needed, etc. These are perfectly advisable, desired, and sensible choices. I'm just saying to learn enough about other modalities to make informed decisions. It really is your choice, and your body, if you want to live longer.

A Holistic Approach to Healthy Skin

Our skin wraps around the bones, muscles, ligaments, and tendons to act as the barrier to keep things out of our body as well as letting things in. The condition of our skin shows what is going on inside the body. It's the largest organ of excretion, as well as a vehicle to transport things inside the body.

What impacts our skin? Well, our lifestyle choices for one—like how much time you spend out in the sun; what you put on your skin; how well you clean it; whether you smoke; your emotional state and how stressed you are; how much exercise you get; the amount of sleep you get; and how you impact your skin from the inside with your diet, supplements, and water intake. If you look at all the factors to see where you might make changes, you can better deal with keeping your face wrinkle-free and looking younger longer.

One of My Best Tools for Health

When it comes to natural health modalities, you have already heard me speak of the essential oils throughout this book. I'd like to talk more about this natural alternative modality, which truly comes from nature and helps in dealing with physical, emotional, and mental health issues.

How many of you know about essential oils? They have been around since the third day of creation when God created the plants, and were used by different cultures all around the world throughout history. They are mentioned throughout the Bible. These are the aromatic liquids that are steam-distilled from plants, trees, bushes, flowers, roots, and seeds, and cold-pressed from citrus rinds, while a few are absolute-alcohol-extracted.

Each plant has hundreds of constituents that give that plant its unique properties. Oils are much more concentrated and potent than dried herbs. The oils are concentrated through a distillation process, which must be particular and precise to each plant so as to not destroy the valuable properties of the plant's essential oils.

Essential oils can be used:

- topically—straight from the bottle or preferably diluted with a carrier oil and applied on the skin where needed;
- aromatically—smelling directly from the bottle or diffusing with a cold air diffuser into the air; and
- internally—those that are able to be taken internally, put in water, juice, tea, or in a capsule. You can also add some oils able to be used internally in foods—just need a drop or two for great taste.

You do want to know the essential oils company you choose and how they grow, process, distill, and test the oils to be sure you are getting pure, therapeutic-grade oils that have a medicinal effect. Quality of the oils is of paramount importance. They need to be distilled in stainless steel containers, using low temperature, low pressure, and sometimes for many hours to extract all the natural chemical compounds. This is important as there may be a toxic compound in the oil, but there will also be a buffering compound that makes it safe to use the oil.

Many tests are conducted to determine what is in the oil, whether all the compounds are present to give the desired effect, and if it's pure and not contaminated with chemicals used in the field or on the plants.

I so appreciate the fact that Young Living doesn't use chemicals for pests or weeds at any point, or use chemicals to pull the oils out faster during the distillation process. They seek to product oils pure enough to have powerful medicinal effect—to be used externally, aromatically, as well as internally. Each oil is put through the full range of tests three times before being sent to you in its sealed bottle.

These are powerful and potent oils, so they must be used with respect and knowledge. You only need a drop or two to have an effect on your body. The safest way is to dilute them with a carrier oil to spread further on the skin and prevent them from feeling too warm or too concentrated. Carrier oils can be coconut oil, extra virgin olive oil, sesame oil, sweet almond oil, walnut oil, etc. These have a large molecular size (1000 amu—atomic mass unit) and don't go through the pores and into the cells as the essential oils can, which are 500 amu's or smaller.

You want to be sure you don't get the oils in your eyes or dripped on your eardrum, as they will burn from the intensity of the oil. Make sure if that happens you dilute the oil with a carrier oil, *not water*, as that will drive it in deeper and intensify the effect of the burning sensation. To use oils in the bathtub, mix a handful of Epsom salts with several drops of the oil, then hold under running water to disperse them throughout the bath.

Benefits of Essential Oils

Those are some facts about essential oils, but the wonderful aspect of them is all the benefits they offer:

- Support healthy body functions and help boost the immune system.
- Relieve discomfort and sore muscles after exercising at the gym or spending time working outside.
- Soothe the digestive system, dealing with indigestion, bloating, gas, cramps, etc.
- Boost your ability to focus and concentrate.
- Make a massage more effective.
- Help you relax and reduce your stress levels enabling better sleep.
- Promote wellness.
- Provide safer and nontoxic ways to clean and purify both home and work spaces.
- Help you achieve healthier skin and great-looking hair.
- Impact emotions in a positive manner by crossing the blood-brain barrier to reach the amygdala and limbic system.
- Plus many other benefits too numerous to list.

Essential Oils and the Body's Systems

Now we'll explore the systems of the body one by one and the essential oils that can help support and strengthen that system. Many books are available to give more specific information about how to use essential oils—how many drops, carrier oils to use, blends to put together, and cautions.

I cannot diagnose, prescribe, or treat anyone, but I can give you some general guidelines to use for the different body systems. I will inform you about common single oils you can get from many different sources, but may I say again that the source of your oils is very important. You want to know if they've been grown without chemicals, how they've been distilled, what tests have been done, and what standards they meet. If you are using them to get a medicinal effect, to see results that have helped your body feel better, then you want to get the best you can find. For me, that is Young Living Essential Oils.

I recommend also getting an essential oils reference guide, which you can find on Amazon. One is *Essential Oils Desk Reference* compiled by Life Science Publishing. Another is *Reference Guide for Essential Oils* by Higley. You don't need both to start out, but having one is definitely a help to find what oils to use for a specific issue you are looking for.

Musculoskeletal System

The first system I want to address is the musculoskeletal system. So many people have issues with joints, muscles, tendons, ligaments, and bones, which are all part of this system. Some essential oils that are helpful with this system: peppermint, Idaho balsam fir, wintergreen, Idaho blue spruce, lavender, helichrysum, marjoram, basil, clove, and nutmeg. Others can also help, but these are enough choices to get you started.

Hormone/Endocrine System

Another system that impacts our whole-body functioning is our hormone/endocrine system. Many of us have hypothyroid issues, weight gain, hair loss, diminished sex drive, sleep issues—and these are all impacted by our endocrine system. Some oils that beneficially impact this system are: frankincense, myrtle, clove, rosemary, geranium, cinnamon bark, lemongrass, myrrh, nutmeg, dill, grapefruit, cedarwood, and fennel.

Digestive System

Another system most of us have issues with is our digestive system. We don't eat enough fiber or take in enough pure water. Therefore our bodies don't properly break down the food so that we get the nutrition from what we do eat. As a result, we often deal with belching, abdominal gas, cramps, heartburn, and bloating. The following are great oils to help your body deal with this: peppermint, tarragon, thyme, wintergreen, ginger, lemon, fennel, oregano, nutmeg, and lemongrass. I put a drop or two under my tongue, dilute a drop or two and rub it all over my belly, or even put a couple drops in water and drink it down. One of these oils can relieve my discomfort in a few minutes, so I always make sure I have it handy.

Cardiovascular System

Another crucial bodily system is our cardiovascular system—heart, blood, veins, and arteries. The heart functions to bring vital oxygen and nutrients throughout the body. Blood removes waste and carbon dioxide from cells, so the body can detoxify itself. Blood also carries important immune cells and hormones. Blood is to the body like an essential oil is to a plant—it acts as the plant's immune system, carries hormones, and moves nutrition into the cells and waste out. Some essential oils to use to promote cardiovascular health: ylang-ylang, wintergreen, rosemary, marjoram, cypress, helichrysum, frankincense, cistus, goldenrod, clove, and orange.

Immune System

Another equally important system is our immune system. Where would we be if our body didn't protect us from all the bacteria, viruses, fungi, and parasites that try to overtake our systems? I find I have been much healthier since I've been using essential oils for the last twenty years. If anything "catches" me, it's usually pretty mild in severity and length. Here are oils that can aid our immune systems: frankincense, oregano, rosemary, lemon, eucalyptus, thyme, orange, melaleuca, clove, lavender, and cinnamon bark.

Respiratory System

Another system we absolutely can't do without is our respiratory system. Aren't you glad that our bodies breathe automatically without us having to remember to take each breath? We'd get worn out trying to take care of the running of each one of our body systems, so God set it up to be run by our autonomic nervous system—automatically. Here are oils that help support the respiratory system: eucalyptus, frankincense, peppermint, lemon, myrtle, melaleuca, Idaho balsam fir, lavender, and myrrh.

Nervous System

Our nervous system is broken down into two parts: the CNS or central nervous system, which includes the brain and spinal cord; and our PNS, or peripheral nervous system, which is comprised of all the other sensory nerves in our fingers, skin, muscles, and organs and which pick up sensations and relay that information to the brain. The brain then decides what to do with it, as in fight, flight, or freeze. Some oils that are supportive and nourishing to our nervous system: cedarwood, Royal Hawaiian sandalwood, Idaho balsam fir, melissa, frankincense, roman chamomile, vetiver, valerian, and lavender.

Excretory System

Our excretory system starts with the large colon, and continues to the end with the anus. Oils helpful for this system are: juniper, lemon, geranium, oregano, fennel, Idaho balsam fir, peppermint, grapefruit, and melaleuca.

Integumentary System

This system sounds like a mouthful—integumentary system—but covers our skin, hair, nails, teeth, ears, and sweat glands. One of the biggest organs of our body is our skin. Just think of everything our skin encounters or that we put on it, and then think about all the chemicals we absorb through the day. So maybe we should be more conscious and aware to start protecting ourselves from this onslaught. Some oils that are protective and helpful for this system are: frankincense, lavender, melaleuca, peppermint, myrrh, geranium, cedarwood, patchouli, melrose, and German chamomile.

Reproductive System

I don't know that I'm as concerned or interested in the reproductive system anymore as I don't know what I'd do with a baby at this age! I'm long past menopause and enjoying the lack of periods and all that having periods entails during all the reproductive years. But . . . for those who are still in those child-bearing years, here are the oils that can be beneficial for balancing reproductive hormones: geranium, Idaho blue spruce, clary sage, ylang-ylang, myrtle, frankincense, joy, and goldenrod.

Chapter 10

Education on Essential Oils

I have listed many oils you may have never heard of, and you may have no idea what they are or what they do. It is beyond the scope of what I can share here to go into great detail on each oil, but you can find information on each oil in one of the reference guides I mentioned or Google it on the Internet. You can also contact me and I would be happy to talk with you and see what would be useful for your own body needs.

I use a software program that helps let the body show its areas of stress, and then find oils and supplements that can aid in bringing areas of stress back into balance. It's called ZYTO Elite software and uses a hand cradle to let your body communicate with the software through contact points.

Along with the ZYTO, I have a software program called EVOX, which gives voice to your emotions as you talk into a microphone. It records your voice energy and plots it on a graph called a Perception Index. That index will then determine frequency signatures that are most useful to you. It then introduces those energetic signatures to your body via the hand cradle as you listen to relaxing music and think about the topic you are discussing.

The EVOX experience opens you to new ways of seeing things through a process called Perception Reframing. Old perceptions that may be stuck and damaging are released and you become free to choose better ways. This moves you to a position of choice rather than reaction. It can be profound because perception creates personal reality.

I like to consult with people to help them find natural, alternative ways to get to optimal health. Optimal health can mean different things to different people and at whatever point they are in life. We talk about things you can do and change to improve your current life situation.

The Final Quarter

There may come a time when you're hit with a health issue that overwhelms you and you don't know what to do. First, talk about it with your doctor; then consider adding a natural health professional who can suggest natural ways to address it; look at it from an emotional standpoint, since your emotions impact you physically; determine ways to manage your stress levels; seek relaxation through praying, meditation, getting out in nature, exercising, and sharing the burden with close friends; look at ways to improve your diet and sleep; choose supplements to support your body; and include some fun in your life. We often get so set in our ways, ruts, and lifestyle that we forget to lighten our hearts and have *fun*! It might be a novel concept for you. Try it. You might like it!

A cheerful heart is good medicine, but a crushed spirit dries up the bones.
—Proverbs 17:22

Chapter 11
What Is Your Legacy?

All good men and women must take responsibility to create legacies that will take the next generation to a level we could only imagine.
—Jim Rohn

Legacy is a word we hear often, especially as we move into the third and fourth quarters of life. But what is legacy exactly? While many people most closely connect it to one's family generational line, legacy is anything handed down from one generation to the next. A retiring company president might leave a *legacy* of honesty and integrity. A teacher may leave a legacy of a love for learning and motivation to succeed to her many students through the years.

My mom left a legacy of her love for people and showing compassion by taking flowers, cookies, homemade jam, and her girls to visit shut-ins. We sometimes rebelled at going, but I can still see her greeting people, kissing the babies, and patting the hands of the old people. No one was a stranger—she would go up to moms with babies in the grocery stores and start talking and loving on them.

I have tried—*honestly I have tried*—to maintain my distance and be cool, but I find myself doing the same things now. I play "eye games" with babies, give hugs to my friends, love on old people, feel like strangers are just friends I haven't met yet—and I love color as my mom did. She left her legacy in me, as well as my other sisters.

I think the whole world is dying to hear someone say, "I love you." I think that if I can leave the legacy of love and passion in the world, then I think I've done my job in a world that's getting colder and colder by the day.
—Lionel Richie

Jim Rohn, the philosopher who left an indelible legacy of time-proven principles and wisdom, shared his secret for making an impact. "You know me, I am a philosopher. I love principles. Yes, actions are great and I talk about them regularly, but the important stuff is what lies underneath—the principles," Rohn says.[9]

Here are the principles he says we must commit to in order to leave the legacy we desire. I've added my comments about each principle as it speaks to me.

1. Life is best lived in service to others.

Life is multi-faceted, but one of the important facets is serving our families, those we work with, and of course, our friends. It can also include those we come into contact with throughout our lifetime.

2. Consider others' interests as important as your own.

When we consider others and do things for them, it keeps us from getting self-focused and self-centered. It brings balance to our lives.

3. Love your neighbor even if you don't like him.

Love is an action verb that means you help or do good for others. You don't necessarily have to like the person to do so, but liking often follows the action as you get to know the person better.

4. Maintain integrity at all costs.

We can't take our riches with us when we die, but we can take our good name and reputation. You want people to remember what an honest and full-of-integrity person you were. Guard your name and reputation by always doing what is right, no matter what it costs you.

5. You must risk in order to gain.

We can risk in many ways in our lives, but if we don't take risks, we won't ever win the prize that comes from taking those risks. If you want to leave a legacy, you have to take risks to gain the prizes, which could be your spouse, your wealth, your lands, your books, your achievements, etc. Gain so that you have something to leave for others, in tangible or intangible ways.

6. You reap what you sow.

If you plant one seed for corn, you will get an ear with many kernels. So you are getting more corn than you sowed. If you give love to someone, it will grow to be more than you gave. If you spend time with someone and invest in that life, it will increase and grow the value of the time you spend with that person. Whatever you invest in others or in business, it will increase. So sow into others to leave a legacy.

7. Hard work is never a waste.

Much is accomplished when you work hard and spend yourself in the effort to better yourself and the circumstances of others. Be known as a hard worker, as it increases your personal value and leaves a legacy for your children to follow.

8. Don't give up when you fail.

A fact of life is that failure is a part of it—that's how we learn what works and what doesn't. Don't be afraid of failure, and don't give up when it happens. Keep on trying until you actually succeed—that too leaves a legacy for your children and others to follow. How many stories can be told of what happened to you and how you persevered that will inspire those coming after you?

9. Don't ever stop in your pursuit of a legacy.

Age is not a reason to stop pursuing achievements. Age might even be a reason to go forward as we now have more time to spend on our passions and interests. Use all that you have learned in your life to serve others, teach others, guide their lives, and impact more people. In this way you leave a legacy not only for your own family but for all those whose lives you touch. You may even accomplish more in this time of life than you did before, so don't stop living. Pursue your passions.

These are core principles to live by if you want to become the kind of person who leaves a lasting legacy.

I love Jim's principles, as they resonate with what I believe about how I want to live my life and what I want to pass on to others. I love number nine, as that is where I am—later in life and still wanting to achieve more.

You make your mark by being true to who you are and letting that be your staple.
—Kat Graham

I may not have a large monetary legacy to leave my kids or mission organizations, but I hope the legacy I leave will be one of *faithfulness* in sticking to a job, project, or passion. I want to be known for being *someone you can count on* to do what they say they will do; doing it with excellence in a timely fashion, and to the satisfaction of the recipient.

I want my family to see me *achieve my dreams*; that I am willing to *stay the course* even when the obstacles seem overwhelming.

I want them to see that *age is not a barrier* to helping others or *traveling to far places* to be a light where there might not be much light.

I think all of us in our fourth quarter of life should seek to:

- not be afraid to *reach out and speak* to strangers; to be *friendly and engaging*; to *shine forth with the spirit* that is within you.
- be *generous* to those in need and give what you are able.
- *be there for family* when they need assistance or *have their back* in crisis situations.
- leave behind the legacy of a *good reputation* of integrity, honesty, and good morals; of being a *hard worker*; of *determination* to stay the course you've laid out; and of *courage* in tough situations.

Most of all, I want to leave a *legacy of love*—for God, my husband, family, and others outside my family circle. Love covers a multitude of sins—mine and theirs.

Your story is the greatest legacy that you will leave to your friends.
It's the longest-lasting legacy you will leave to your heirs.
—Steve Saint

Leave Your Spiritual Legacy

Our legacy is our story. And our story is what is left after we leave this earth. Stories connect us to others, to the past and the future. They contain common bonds with others. Legacy is not about our stuff, but a desire to leave behind something for others when we die.

"Our spiritual legacy is who we are at our core. What becomes more and more important as we age is the desire to be known—known for who we really were during our brief stay here. What might be one of the saddest things is to leave this earth without those you love the most ever really knowing who you were.

"At the heart of everyone's sacred story is how we have shown, felt, received, and given love in our lives. It is about the compassion, the kindness, the courage, and the beauty that has come into our lives and that has flowed from us but yet remained within us, despite, and because of, all the difficulties and challenges we have endured. It is the story of our soul."[10]

What seeds are you planting? You may never see the fruit of them, but the fact that you planted is part of your legacy. Have you ever considered how others will remember you—most especially your family, grandkids, and great grandkids? What do you want to be remembered for, and how will they remember you—with much love and thankfulness for the impact you had on their lives, or grateful that you are gone? Decide now on the legacy you will leave.

Your physical legacy will pass away, but your spiritual legacy will have eternal impact. You may not have had children; your children may have preceded you in death; you may not have married and become part of another family—but if you have worked or had friends or been part of a church family, you too will leave a legacy with them. We all leave a legacy with someone. So decide how you want to be remembered and live your life accordingly—no matter your circumstances.

Chapter 11

Five Ways to Leave a Great Legacy

As I am in the last quarter of my life, I have started thinking more about the legacy I am leaving for my kids, grandkids, and great grandkids. Our sons are in their late forties, so the desire for a legacy is touching all of us.

Having gone on mission trips for over eleven years to Africa, the Amazon, and Peru makes me different from most grandmas, and the fact that I care about so many people who are different from us culturally makes me almost an anomaly in our circles of friends.

Our kids and grandkids are proud of what I do, and what their grandpa is doing in building a water resource authority from the ground up. They think we are neat. And here we are in our mid-seventies, still going strong. Our grandsons want to travel with me when I go to Kenya to see what I do and what other cultures are like.

The legacy I'm leaving for them is having a heart for people and being willing to step outside my comfort zone to minister health through natural means to them, even if it means traveling halfway around the world year after year, and now several times a year. This speaks volumes without me having to say a word.

"The idea of leaving a legacy is the need or the desire to be remembered for what you have contributed to the world. In some cases, that contribution can be so special that the universe is unalterably changed. However, for most mere mortals walking this earth, most will leave a more modest legacy that doesn't necessarily change the world but does leave a lasting footprint that will be remembered by those whose lives you touched."[11]

I hope my life has mattered to someone in some way, and that I have impacted someone's health and well-being, as well as their heart. I became a nurse at the age of twenty, and have been touching people's bodies and hopefully their hearts ever since. I have learned natural ways to deal with health that don't cause harmful side effects and have used essential oils and basic health care to deal with health needs all over the world. I have taught many others to do the same so they could carry on when I wasn't there, using the tools I left with them.

My family is the reason I want to leave a legacy—for our two sons, five grandkids, and one great-granddaughter. I also have three dear and loving sisters, along with their husbands, who are very much a part of my life.

In an online article, Joan Moran speaks of five ways to leave a great legacy.[12] I like these ideas and have shared below each one what they mean to me:

1. Support the people and causes that are important to you.

A number of my friends are missionaries in the countries where they have chosen to live and work with the local people in their day-to-day lives, and also teach them about the Lord. As I've spent time with them, watching all they do and the things they deal with that are so different from our lives in America, I am impressed with the dedication and fervor with which they pour out their lives to serve others. I desire to support them in their efforts and monetarily help them so they can stay where they are, usually serving without pay from the places they serve. Monies have to come from those who are back home believing in their efforts and willing to donate funds to them.

2. Reflect and decide what is most important in your life.

From a very young age I desired to serve others through nursing, so that became what I studied and learned how to do—nursing, giving anesthesia, at one point in my life working with the deaf and learning sign language to communicate with them, learning about essential oils and teaching others about them, and then going on mission trips to share those skills and knowledge. To touch others' lives is important to me.

3. Share your blessings with others.

My life is full of blessings: family—love of them and from them—friends who add a rich dimension, a long and interesting career in medicine, the ability to travel and meet so many others who impact my life, and mentors who taught me business and social media skills. I have been abundantly blessed and desire to pour into others the things I have been given. They increase in value when you pass the blessings on.

4. Be a mentor to others.

One of the joys of life is to share all your expertise with those who want to learn what you know. You help them expand their scope of understanding and gain experience as they grow. You support them along the way, as it is a process that takes time and effort. The relationships that develop can last a lifetime as you pour your heart and soul into them, which they can then turn around and "do unto others as you have done unto them."

5. Pursue your passions because they are infectious.

"Your passions are your legacy," said Moran. "Passion comes from an outpouring of the interests and ideas that make a difference in your life. Finding and pursing your passion allows you to see your destiny clearly. That's what happened to me with yoga and dancing tango. I can attest to the fact that life won't be any fun if you don't pursue your passions to the fullest. It's contagious. It's religious.

Don't miss the opportunity to pursue your passions and then continue to look for new adventures.

"Leaving a legacy is an important part of your life's work. A legacy develops from a life dedicated to self-reflection and purpose. What will be revealed and what will endure is a truthful and value-driven body of living."[13]

When I learned about essential oils and the impact they can have on people, I became more and more passionate about them. As the years went by and I gained more experience and saw some tremendous outcomes from using the oils, I knew I couldn't keep quiet about this treasure God had given us from the earth. Through all the defining moments of my life ran this thread of service and love using God's tool.

Carve your name on hearts, not tombstones. A legacy is etched into the minds of others and the stories they share about you.
—Shannon L. Alder

Leaving a Legacy

I have fought the good fight, I have finished the race,
I have kept the faith.
2 Timothy 4:7

Do you ever wonder what kind of legacy you'll leave behind?

My father was a pastor who ministered in the pulpit until he was brought down by Parkinson's and developing dementia. He loved to share about Jesus all his life, and I'm sure he impacted many people as he pastored in the churches where he served. He died at eighty-eight and left his legacy of loving Jesus in his four girls, as well as those whose lives he touched.

Chapter 11

My mom died when she was ninety. She spent eight years alone after Daddy died, but never stopped playing the piano or organ, which she was gifted at doing. The night before she died of a heart attack found her playing the organ for the people who lived with her in an assisted living home. She taught piano and organ to many students over the years, and taught music theory as well. Her love of people, flowers, color, and music was her legacy to us and it lives on in us girls as well. She kept on doing everything she loved right to the end.

That example inspires me, as I want to be found with my boots on right up to the end—going to others and ministering with hands of love—usually with oils on them! I want to be found faithful in following Christ, fighting the good fight for the faith he left us, and finish the race of life still qualified to be called a Christ-follower. That means I have to keep my spiritual armor on to protect myself from the attacks of the enemy—Satan—who wants to discourage and get me off track. I have to put aside all the lures of the world, the things that call to me, that entice me to step aside and try them, and which would take my eyes off following Jesus.

If this happens to you as well, God will keep putting signs in front of you, give you messages every place you look, have friends send you words to call you back, and use circumstances to tap you on the shoulder. If He has given you a work to do, He will help you overcome the enemy and come back into His fold. He is jealous for our love and attention.

I want to be found faithful. So every day is a choice as to what gets my attention and focus. As Paul told the Philippians, "Forgetting what is behind and straining toward what is ahead, I press on toward the goal to win the prize for which God has called me heavenward in Christ Jesus" (Philippians 3:13–14).

Each one of us can decide today to leave behind a legacy that can impact others. When you make a decision, consider what it will do to influence the minds and hearts of those you love. Will it be positive or negative? Do you need to make some changes to move back into a legacy of faithful service to Christ?

I'm so thankful God is willing to give us His grace to forgive us, cleanse our hearts, and help us refocus. He can take the time you have left here on this earth to bring glory and honor to Him. And that should be our bottom line—His glory.

I have shared principles and points from several authors as their words impacted me. Their thoughts on legacy resonated within me and brought forth thoughts from within myself that I shared with you. I hope these insights have made you think about your own legacy. It's not a topic you hear talked about enough but it really can and will impact lives all around you.

Now that we've thought about the impact and legacy we want to leave, we need to address how we are going to finish this last quarter well. I will tell you how I want to finish it and give you some thoughts about completing your final quarter.

Chapter 12
Finishing Well

On one of our rambling, exploring drives around the mountains of north Georgia, we found a big old building in which many people had booths to sell their treasures. I found a plaque that piqued my interest and sparked something inside me, so I bought it and hung it above one of the doorways in my upstairs office.

As I began work on this chapter, it was raining, so I took time out for a nap and fell asleep to the sound of rain. What a lovely moment, and so relaxing! As I woke up from my nap, I lay there contemplating what I wanted to share about how to "finish well," and my eyes fell on this sign. It seemed to echo my thoughts:

Live like you'll never be hurt.
Sing like no one is listening.
Dance like no one is watching.
Live like it's heaven on earth.

Now, we know people are all around us and may see what we are doing, but I think the point to these simple lines is to lose our inhibitions, shyness, and reticence and express ourselves freely; to live life to the fullest and not let the opinions and negativity of others stop us from enjoying life.

The Final Quarter

Finishing My Life Well

As I ponder this suggestion to live a free and full life, I have to hold the mirror up to myself. And when I do, I see a woman who is learning to let go and enjoy life as it was intended—full of joy and wonder.

For so many years, I lived an inhibited life because I was self-conscious a about how I looked and because I was raised to be prim and proper. Not to say that I'm all that uninhibited now, but I have learned to be more expressive, to let go and enjoy life, to laugh and love others, and to express my friendship with them. I also am more willing to reach out for help and guidance, where before I tried to do everything myself and was often frustrated with the results.

I am even learning to accept that I'm beautiful—both inside and out—because God made me to look the way I do—and He doesn't make junk!

I'm confident that I *do* have a lot to give to people from all I've learned in my many years of experience in the medical field, and all the studying I've done on essential oils and alternative health. I see my value in my love for missions and my desire to impact others around the world, using a tool from God for their health issues, as well as showing His love for them as I apply the essential oils with my hands.

I love traveling and am still healthy and flexible enough to put up with the long flights, long drives, and hours of working.

I am so thankful that we have two beautiful sons and their families to love on and support. We have enjoyed some great family trips out west where we have made memories that last a lifetime.

As I mentioned earlier, I want to keep on being, doing, going, sharing, traveling, growing spiritually, and helping others in ways they need, and loving with a stronger passion than ever before.

Chapter 12

How to Finish Well

I want to burn out, not rust out! I want to make every minute of my life count and not waste it. Life is too precious for that. How can *you* live *your* life to the fullest?

Look at your life holistically—meaning from every angle—and see how you can improve areas that will impact your spiritual, mental, emotional, and physical self. Change any negative and harmful practices. Lose the chemicals; reduce the EMF impacts; improve your diet and what you drink; incorporate chemical-free essential oils to support all your body systems; take supplements that contain oils to benefit your body; read the owner's manual for your body and life—called the Bible—which will give you answers on living your life; connect with friends and family in a deeper, more loving way; find your dreams and passions and resurrect them again. Start pursuing those desires and goals—revive your zest for living so you want to get up in the mornings.

Think about some of the things you have wanted to do in the past—take a river cruise on the Rhine in Europe; go zip-lining; travel the Mississippi River on a steamboat; see the White Mountains in New England in the fall; rent a houseboat and live on the lake for a week; take a hot-air balloon ride; see the Grand Canyon; take up knitting, quilting, crocheting, or other artwork with fabrics; paint—either your house or pictures; do volunteer work; take weekend mini-vacations with a friend or two; go to concerts, enjoy nature walks, go whale-watching in New England; rent a cabin in the mountains with friends and just breathe the fresh mountain air, etc. Getting back to nature is invigorating and refreshing for the soul. Discovering new passions and restoring your dreams from the past is a great way to finish well and leave a legacy of memories.

The Final Quarter

Find ways to get outside of your comfort zone or the rut you have allowed yourself to get into. Many things don't cost a lot of money, so don't use that as an excuse. Nature is one way to experience joy without spending a dime. It's right outside your door. And even if you're unable to move freely, you can enjoy nature through your window, or even through beautiful photographs. Don't let any limitations keep you from discovering the many ways to enjoy this last quarter.

Live outside yourself—don't focus on the aches and pains that slow you down. Get outside, walk, and breathe. Practice gratitude for all that surrounds you. Live as though you are alive—up to the moment you leave this world and go to the next.

Life may try to beat you down with tragedies and disasters and lack of health, finances, or possessions, but it can't kill the spark of life in each of us. If you can't blow on that spark, let someone else fan the flame and give you the oxygen to make it burn brighter to help you come back to full life. "No man is an island," it is said, and we are here to help carry one another's burdens.

A saying on Facebook caught my attention:

At the end of life, what really matters is not what we bought but what we built;
Not what we got, but what we shared;
Not our competence, but our character.
Live a life of love.

The greatest love we can live and share in our lives comes from our Creator. If you don't know that personally, I encourage you to decide now where you want to spend eternity and make the changes necessary to spend it with our Maker and Creator—God.

Chapter 12

How beautifully leaves grow old. How full of light and color are their last days.
—John Burroughs

Your final quarter—make it memorable, glorious, impacting, shining, and a treasure in this earthen vessel that will be pleasing to God.

To laugh often and much;
to win the respect of intelligent people
and the affection of children,
to leave the world a better place,
to know even one life has breathed easier
because you have lived,
this is to have succeeded.
—Ralph Waldo Emerson

Notes

1. Dr. Myles Munroe, as quoted by Mayona Tijani, "'The wealthiest place on earth is the cemetery' and other memorable Myles Munroe quotes," The Cable, November 10, 2014, https://www.thecable.ng/wealthiest-place-earth-cemetery-%E2%94%80-memorable-munroe-quotes.

2. Jack Tatar, "5 Biggest Regrets of Retirees," Market Watch, December 10, 2013, https://www.marketwatch.com/story/5-biggest-regrets-by-retirees-2013-12-10/email.

3. Bronnie Ware, *The Top Five Regrets of the Dying; A Life Transformed by the Dearly Departed,* reprint ed. (Carlsbad, CA: Hay House, 2012).

4. Jessica Hatcher, "The Masai Mara: 'It will not be long before it's gone,'" The Guardian, August 23, 2013, https://www.theguardian.com/travel/2013/aug/23/masai-mara-tourism-politics.

5. Fritz Chery, "Being Still," Bible Reasons, January 1, 2018, https://biblereasons.com/being-still/.

6. Dr Joseph Mercola, "Use of Antidepressants Continue to Rise," Mercola, August 31, 2017, http://articles.mercola.com/sites/articles/archive2017/08/31/antidepressant-use-continues-rise.aspx.

7. Tara Spires-Jones, "Single people twice as likely to develop dementia," I News, October 27, 2017, https://inews.co.uk/news/health/single-people-double-risk-of-dementia-study/.

8. Hazel Spencer, "We Live in Heaven," Hazel Rose Looms, April 26, 2018, https://hazelroseloomsblog.wordpress.com/.

9. Jim Rohn, "This Is How You Leave a Legacy," Success, June 17, 2014, https://www.success.com/article/rohn-this-is-how-you-leave-a-legacy.

10. "Leave Your Spiritual Legacy," Life Story Commons, accessed July 20, 2018, usm.maine.edu, http://usm.maine.edu/lifestorycenter/legacy.html.

11. Joan Moran, "5 Ways to Leave a Great Legacy," Huffington Post, April 27, 2015, updated December 6, 2017, https://www.huffingtonpost.com/joan-moran/5-ways-to-leave-a-great-l_b_7148112.html.

12. Ibid.

13. Ibid.

About the Author

Sue Heath is a retired nurse anesthetist, and missionary nurse to the Amazon, Peru, Kenya, and Uganda for the last twelve years. As an entrepreneur dedicated to helping others increase wellness, she teaches people about a healthy way to deal with many physical issues using essential oils, ZYTO scans, Raindrop Technique, consultations, and teaching tours. In her missionary work, she not only assists in health clinics and uses essential oils to help the patients but also trains locals to administer the oils themselves.

Sue is an author, speaker, and international teacher on health; and also an RN, a certified registered nurse anesthetist, an advanced registered nurse practitioner, and a certified natural health professional. Underlying it all, she shares her passion for health and essential oils from a heart that loves the Lord. Her greatest purpose is to serve God by serving others. She is a wife of over fifty years, a mother of two sons, grandmother of five, and great-grandmother of one.

Sue would be grateful to hear from you. You can contact her at sueheath@earthlink.net or www.naturalhealthawakening.com.

Made in the USA
San Bernardino, CA
31 October 2018